MW00716453

"Luke O'Neil's *Welcome* [
of essays on modern Ame..... ....
—*Longreads*

"Reading his popular, semi-weekly newsletter Hell World is a lot like staring deep into O'Neil's soul, and it's often a pretty dark place. Hell World is unusual, to say the least. It's a mix of reporting, essay-writing, memoir, song lyrics, music videos, tweets, and whatever else appeals to him in a given week, all of it written in a stream-of-consciousness style that eschews commas, leans into run-on sentences, and is often thousands of words long. It can get grim, but it's incisive in a way most other newsletters aren't."

—*Boston Magazine*

For your friend who laments the death of alt-weeklies. O'Neil packages his columns in stream-of-consciousness reports that detail the many reasons reasonable people have to be angry right now.

—*New York* Magazine

"Reading "Hell World" can feel like peeling back your eyelids and forcing yourself to watch current events veer toward dystopia, with particular attention to the ugliest and most inhumane details. It's often an uncomfortable read. But if you're aligned with O'Neil's views, it might also force you to face your own discomfort and ask yourself if you're doing enough to reform or dismantle the institutions responsible for the stories he covers."

—WBUR

Welcome To Hell World is a fever dream of a newsletter from Luke O'Neil. It is a random assortment of political musings, links, information and some of the messiest style and syntax — in a good way — you've ever seen in a professional product. It's a lot to handle, but it's great.

—*InsideHook*

"Luke tells it like it is. He is not afraid to take to task the establishment gatekeepers of the world, whether they be police chiefs, democratic politicians, the corporate heads of his own industry, or just your standard Republican bootlickers. It's that honesty, along with pure writing ability, creativity, and a heavy helping of empathy, that makes Luke's writing so special."

—*The Alternative*

His book, adapted from a popular newsletter of the same name (and carrying the subtitle "Dispatches from the American Dystopia"), collects a deluge of horror stories from the American present — opioid addiction and police brutality and crowdfunded healthcare and rampant racism and literal "baby jails" and everything else — injustices that O'Neil takes it upon himself to consume. ...*Welcome to Hell World* is written in a conversational, stream-of-consciousness style that manages to be at once scathingly ironic and disarmingly sincere.... Is it a stretch to call O'Neil an optimist? Not because he thinks he can change this cruel world but that he at least still thinks the injustice is worth recording. Still worth marvelling over in total horror. Still registering surprise that some people, often through nothing more than by being born in a certain place to certain parents, get to weigh up human lives according to the money they stand to lose or gain.

—*Full Stop*

As Boston polemicist Luke O'Neil writes in the first book named for his popular newsletter (and subtitled *Dispatches from the American Dystopia*), in a chapter exploring his thoughts about the annual Veteran's Day display on Boston Common: "The flags looked beautiful I have to admit but I don't know why we make war memorials look good they should look terrible. A war memorial should be a guy with his guts hanging out crying for his mother or a guy without a leg getting denied mental health services at the VA. People want things to be like what they think they are like unless it's war in which case they want it to look like a TV show." We feel the same way about writings on contemporary matters, from politics to music—they should be beautiful but hideous at the same time—and O'Neil scratches that itch for a remarkable 538 pages.

—*Dig Boston*

"Writer Luke O'Neil explores the fear and violence of daily life in mid-collapse USA - on the wrong side of class lines, regular people are sold war overseas and paranoia at home by a media and political class with no real [involvement] besides collecting profit and floating high above the chaos they sow."

—*This Is Hell! Radio*

In the foreword to *Welcome to Hell World*, Luke O'Neil admits that he does not know what his book is. It covers a lot: loneliness and addiction in all their forms, absurdity and cruelty and how they're often paired together, people as soft matter shredded by this nation's exploitative systems. The collection hits upon all the major works in the canon of Americanness: opioid addiction, the border wall, climate change, pollution, the healthcare system, police violence, mass shootings, etc.

And just as important is the gaze on them—how the reddest brutalities are smoothed down by corporatized language, or shouted over by hysterical pleas for civility, refracted through social media and its churn, or blown up by CNN or MSNBC's fluorescent newsroom. As I read it, O'Neil hasn't declared this a "hell world" just because there are a bunch of terrible and ruthless systems that ravage people's lives. It's also about how people try to position themselves morally to justify these systems, and how they are conditioned to treat even the most powerless people with a kind of cutting, hypocritical moral absolutism.

—*Protean Magazine*

LOCKDOWN IN HELL WORLD

LOCKDOWN
IN
HELL WORLD

LUKE O'NEIL

O/R

OR Books

New York · London

© 2021 Luke O'Neil

Published by OR Books, New York and London
Visit our website at www.orbooks.com

All rights information: rights@orbooks.com

First printing 2020

Cataloging-in-Publication data is available from the Library of Congress.
A catalog record for this book is available from the British Library.

Typeset by Lapiz Digital Services. Printed by BookMobile, USA, and CPI, UK.

paperback ISBN 978-1-68219-408-9 • ebook ISBN 978-1-68219-245-0

I reached under the bed for my menthols
and she asked if I ever thought of cancer.

Yes, I said, but always as a tree way up ahead
in the distance where it doesn't matter
– David Berman, "Imagining Defeat"

CONTENTS

IT'S LIKE A FUCKING HORROR MOVIE THAT NEVER ENDS

Jesus Christ this dude even has to lose weird. I decided to wait to see what happened with the election before finally and irrevocably finishing this book and sending it off into the remainder bins and full satisfaction has yet to arrive. It's like a José Saramago novel where everyone in the country suddenly has to sneeze all at once but we just can't do it and we all live imprisoned in that hesitation indefinitely. Or a better analogy than that. All this month it's felt like waiting to find out what kind of cancer we've got meanwhile one of our doctors is crying that the MRI is rigged. I don't know man I can't think straight I haven't had a normal hour since the election which was roughly four years ago as best as I can tell. If this has been a year of the neverending March this month has been one continuous and interminable election day. It's the sort of purgatory this diseased and spiraling country deserves.

I nonetheless will be happy to see Trump finally and utterly and officially lose. Although "Joe Biden is president now" will feel so much less good than "Donald Trump is president again" would have felt bad if you follow me there. It's like the emotional ceiling of a Biden win is a modest ranch home and the emotional basement of a Trump win is the cursed tunnel from *Annihilation*.

It's also all pretty funny though. Biden is not going to improve many of our lives in any material way but watching Donald Trump the worst man we have produced in decades speed-running through the stages of grief and trapped in a constant state of having just lost and always being just about to lose is delightful.

As we're waiting violent rallies to "stop the steal" have begun as Trump insists the election was fixed—which he also did for some reason in the last one he actually won—and I guess at this point our best case scenario is Trump flags becoming the next lost cause symbol and contractors with $50,000 trucks terrorizing us with them for the next twenty years until the climate becomes too terrible to remember anything that happened more than a week previously and then we're all dead anyway.

I'm not stupid (citation needed) but there was at least a small part of me that hoped as I was writing this book that by the time it came out we might at least have some vague glimmer of hope on the horizon for the pandemic ending but where we stand now is worse than it has ever been. The past week in mid-November we recorded one million new cases of coronavirus for the first time and we're breaking new records for infections and deaths every day. There is still no stimulus coming and no nationwide mask mandate and no clear guidance on what to do from anyone besides governors scolding us for getting together with friends while keeping bars and gyms and salons open. The virus can't spread when you're spending money apparently. Just this week a case of the virus was reported on a cruise ship—the first to set sail in the Caribbean since the pandemic began—and it's had to go immediately into lockdown. We're at the point where history is rhyming already and the first note of the song hasn't even resolved yet. Thanksgiving and Christmas are approaching and people everywhere including the good ones like you are going to travel to see your stupid fucking families and eat some shitty turkey and bring the virus back home to wherever you came from. I just saw a headline from the Mississippi Free Press: After Big Thanksgiving Dinners, Plan Small Christmas Funerals.

I also just saw a thread on Twitter from a nurse named Jodi Doering in South Dakota a state that is currently being pummeled by infections although I guess they all are right now it's just a matter of degree.

"I have a night off from the hospital," she wrote. "As I'm on my couch with my dog I can't help but think of the Covid patients the last few days. The ones that stick out are those who still don't believe the virus is real. The ones who scream at you for a magic medicine and that Joe Biden is going to ruin the USA. All while gasping for breath on 100% Vapotherm. They tell you there must be another reason they are sick. They call you names and ask why you have to wear all that 'stuff' because they don't have Covid because it's not real."

"Yes. This really happens. And I can't stop thinking about it. These people really think this isn't going to happen to them. And then they stop yelling at you when they get intubated. It's like a fucking horror movie that never ends.

There's no credits that roll. You just go back and do it all over again."

Then I watched a video from a nurse named Lawanna Rivers working in El Paso. She said patients in the hospital there—where they've currently got ten mobile morgues set up and are using inmate labor to move the bodies—are being left to die.

"What I saw there this past month was horrific," she said near tears in a video that soon went viral. "For some reason the doctors there did not aggressively treat the Covid patients."

"I saw a lot of people die that I feel like shouldn't have died. Y'all that assignment there broke me. I was put in what was called 'a pit.' It was eight patients. I was told whatever patients go into the pit they only come out in a body bag."

Because they had Covid she said the policy was they would only get three rounds of CPR. Six minutes of attempting to save their lives. Not a single patient that coded during her shifts made it out alive.

"If those doctors there would aggressively treat those patients from the beginning a lot more would make it," she said. "The nurse that orientated me had one patient, she was called the 'VIP' patient, she was a doctor's wife. And when I say they pulled out all the stops for that woman . . . It was nothing that they didn't do for that woman, and guess what, she was the one patient that made it out of that ICU alive."

I've been running a series in the Hell World newsletter called The Last Normal Day where a bunch of my friends and favorite writers contribute essays about the time just before the pandemic became real for them. They've all been beautiful but this bit from Joe Keohane feels apropos to quote from here.

It's been said before the Covid-19 exploited some key American vulnerabilities: an individualism that can be indistinguishable from pathological selfishness. A society that moves around a lot. And, of course, a government ruled by vandals, paranoids, and dead-enders. But for me one of the hidden vulnerabilities was our national addiction to a certain idea of heroism. James Baldwin wrote this about cops during a protest march: 'There they stood in twos and threes and fours, in their Cub Scout uniforms and with their Cub Scout faces, totally unprepared, as is the way with most American he-men, for anything that could not be settled with a club, or a fist, or a gun.

The coronavirus crisis was incompatible with American hero mythology, with our idea of action. We simply did not have the psychological tools to cope with something that would not respond to violence, threats, or bombast. You couldn't kick its ass, or root for the army to kick its ass, or even console yourself with fantasies of kicking its ass yourself--that sad but enduring Walter Mitty man-saves-the-day fantasy that I suspect provides much of the drive of the American male's love for guns. No, with Covid there was no comfort in violent fantasy. You couldn't do anything. You really could only do nothing. In fact, for the vast majority of us, nothing was the thing you had to do. And the country failed spectacularly, and 2020 feels like the year that will never end.

On Sunday morning the day after the election had finally been called for Biden in the media although long before Trump had conceded which as of this writing he still has not done there came a sound like a tossed orange bruising against the side of my house. Was that a . . . bird? Michelle asked and I said hmm? because I was wallowing and not present at the time which is my way. I climbed from the floor over to the front window which had been my perch this summer while searching for signs of a neighbor gardening murderously and not finding anything remarkable I went back to my business which as I mentioned is a lugubrious idle a sort of sustained and poorly struck 17 hour long A-minor chord that diminishes only for the refrain of restless sleep.

Not long after news started to arrive of an earthquake in Massachusetts which they said originated in Buzzards Bay into which we had fanned my father's ashes one day in the cold spitting rain a few years ago. Earthquakes in Massachusetts are not exactly a common occurrence and while many people reported feeling it I did not.

I watched as people very close to where I live and all over New England shared stories about the ground moving in various degrees of severity and it felt like I was missing out like we were robbed of the experience. Not that I have any desire to know what an actual devastating earthquake is like obviously but to have felt something that powerful for once in my life would have been interesting at the very least. Something different. It snowed six inches here on Halloween the other day which immediately melted when we shifted to a week of 75 degree days in November so why not an earth-quake too?

All throughout that weekend people in cities large and small around the country danced in the streets and honked their horns and struck drums with joy and blasted YG and Miley Cyrus and hugged and cried and for brief pockets I too felt something like what they felt but I couldn't make it stay. I yelled out to the postman on Saturday and we raised our fists together and he said something like "after all that shit he said about us!" and I tried the stunt again later when I saw some neighbors out front but they were mostly concerned with doing yard work or at least didn't feel inclined to share any of their hypothetical jubilance with me in particular. I jogged down to the tiny little town green where a small crowd had gathered waving signs and I hooted with them briefly then ran on past the mailbox-sized woman who's been waving an enormous Trump flag all month and for the first time since the height of the anti-police brutality protests I felt a longing to live closer to the city again as if I was missing out on com-munity to exult with. And then I thought about it a bit more and realized I didn't particularly feel like partying at all.

To be sure I despise Donald Trump and his coterie of sulfurous worms as much as the corniest Joy Reid-ass lib and I am pleased to see him have his pants pulled down to his ankles but this is a moment I've been anticipating with a mixture of hope and dread almost every single day for four years and now that it's finally here I feel no overriding or perspective-shifting sense of catharsis. In fact right now things seem worse than ever as we've been trapped in a transitionary period where Trump and Biden are both currently the president and the loser so we're getting to experience the worst of both worlds at once. Trump is still lying constantly and threatening to further corrupt and abuse what's left of the husks of our institutions and his hordes are caterwauling and trying to claw a somehow even funnier type of defeat out of the jaws of normal defeat — and as stupid and ineffectual as they are how confident are you in this current climate that they won't be able to pull something out of their asses that at the very last prolongs this purgatory? — and thus I do take some solace in their weird despondency but things like spite and schadenfreude can only buoy one's spirit to a certain degree in the way a candy bar will give you a boost of energy before a sugar crash.

On the plus side none of us could have ever possibly written anything as funny as Rudy Giuliani bringing a sex offender as a witness to a landscaping service on the outskirts of Philly next to a crematorium and a dildo shop to lie about voter fraud only to be told in the middle of his speech that everyone had called it for Trump. We'll always have that.

Almost immediately thereafter the centrists that foisted Biden upon us including pharma hogs like Clyburn and CIA ghouls like Spanberger and general catch-all fucking losers like Shalala and McCaskill and Kasich all began sharpening the cutlery with which they intend to shiv the progressive left the very people who willed this probably pyrrhic victory into shape and have pushed all along for massively popular concepts that could conceivably help people like a Green New Deal and Medicare for All and legal marijuana and defunding the police and a $15+ minimum wage. Do you have any reason to believe any of those things are forthcoming in a Biden administration?

And yet I listen to the most committed of activists who labored to make these shifts possible in Michigan and Pennsylvania and Georgia who counsel to take solace in the small victories so you can remember what they felt like as things get harder later on and that gets me halfway back to relief. They know better than I do. The normie lib and the cynical leftist are locked in battle in my brain and I don't think that antagonism is going to go away any time soon. It feels like getting into an argument on Twitter with a reply guy that's actually you running your own alt-account. Like many of us I certainly have some leftover ingrained lib brain damage I have had to take pains to chop away at like overgrown brush over the years. That shit takes maintenance. I wonder if in so doing I've poisoned anything in me that's capable of feeling optimistic along the way or if instead I should finally and utterly strangle that dude to death?

I keep going outside in the middle of writing a sentence and smoking a cigarette I neither want nor need as if I'm going to find the answer to how to finish this out there by staring at the truck in my neighbor's driveway.

I tweeted that a bird had flown into the house like a big fucking idiot and asked if seismic shit like an earthquake could mess up their radar or whatever and a bird-lover quoted me to dunk on me writing "when you are entitled (and ignorant) enough to think that birds hit windows on purpose . . ." which is honestly a hilarious thing to be owned for on Twitter. I guess I got my answer anyway. It couldn't really tell the ground from the sky for a minute and it crashed.

In any case I apologize to all birds everywhere. I should not have maligned their character like that.

It's so newly warm out the bees have returned and they're hovering around listlessly inspecting the dead flowers their instincts tell them should be verdant like when the potluck has winded down but you're poking around the congealed remains for one last tepid meatball. One bee decided to give me a closer look and I waved away at it lazily but it was so weak my swat knocked it to the ground where it stayed and I felt bad about it but not as bad as I would have if it was still trying to sting me.

I don't know.

The sun feels nice here and there on my face but it's a false spring. It's giving me reason for hope but it's fleeting. It's better than an eternal frost I suppose. Things can always become much worse. I wonder if they can ever become better.

WE'RE ROUNDING THE TURN, WE'RE ROUNDING THE CORNER, IT'S GOING AWAY

He didn't die. He didn't fucking die. Motherfucker. It's the middle of October now about a month since I turned in the final draft of this book and so much has happened you could write an entire other book about it but I'm not going to do that because I have had quite enough of the writing of books at the moment. Just the first week of the month alone was an endless onslaught of news most notable of which was our strongman president's dozens of bungling infected henchmen puking and shitting deadly disease all over each other slipping and skating down the diarrhea covered halls of the White House like an ice slick sidewalk. But then he didn't die. None of them died. Not even Chris Christie and that one seemed like a freebie. This is of course because the rich and powerful are afforded a level of medical care that the rest of us can only dream of. Meanwhile the number of deaths has risen over 220,000 and Joe Biden is still at this late date talking about ensuring everyone has "access" to healthcare. Even in the best case scenario no help is forthcoming.

The other week I hit a low point when I saw ol' Donny No Breath standing on the White House balcony barking out poison from his hopefully rapidly scarring lungs while saluting a departing helicopter shortly after having been released from the hospital and I realized I had crashed after a few days of excitement during which I let myself start to think that this horrific pig dick of a man might actually face one single and uniquely ironic consequence. I should've known better. I guess Rachel Maddow and the rest of the civility libs prayed too hard for his speedy recovery which was a whole thing we were arguing about there for a while remember that? In any case no comeuppance will be presently arriving unless he loses the election in humiliating fashion which is information you people reading this now have and I do not. What's the future like?

In the beginning of all this I used to go haha what day is it? as like a bit but now I just say what day is it? flatly and without any sort of levity behind it. When you first gain ten pounds you might go haha I'm getting a little thick over here as a means of deflection but if you keep on gaining weight you stop joking about it and that's just how you are now. Michelle told me just now it was Friday and it made no difference to me one way or the other like when you walk into a room and someone is watching a baseball game you don't care about and you ask the score just to ask something. Like when you meet someone's child and go oh how old are they? but you don't care you just don't know how else to speak to people.

One still even now likes to know the name of the day in any case it's like when it's still dark and silent out and you reach for the wall or the dresser on your way to the bathroom and so then there you are and you know what you're bracketed by. A landmark of a kind.

That reaching out in the dark happens for me more regularly now since I go to bed so early and wake up so early and lately it's pitch black when I do both but I refuse to turn on a light in the morning it feels like a defeat of sorts and so I go and sit on the porch and have my cigarette in the dark in the same spot I had one in the dark eight or nine hours earlier and if you don't actively pay attention you can lose track of which end of the telescope you're looking through.

I've been in the middle of one my famous attempts to "get my shit together" and "take it easy" the past couple of weeks which is a task that seems all the more pointless with nowhere to be and nothing to necessitate having oneself held together for but on the plus side I've managed to start finishing books again which is a lot easier to do when you can wind down into sleep over the course of a couple hours as opposed to being cold-cocked into darkness by a haymaker that comes from inside your own brain. Think of the difference between a leaf drifting slowly to the ground on the wind and an air conditioner being pushed out of a window.

Recently reports have come out about how Kirstjen Nielsen and Rod Rosenstein and Steven Miller and them made child separation at the border an objective and purposeful part of their plan for deterring migrants which is something we all knew but didn't know know and then a couple weeks later it was reported that civil rights lawyers cannot find the parents of at least 545 children we snatched at the border so one thing I want to know at long last is this: Is it ok for me to piss in these monsters' fucking food yet?

Elsewhere some eight million or so have "slipped into poverty" as *The New York Times* put it which sounds almost cute like uh oh I tripped and now I'm homeless and no second stimulus support for actual people has been passed yet and we're almost eight months into this thing now.

I understand logically by the way that the days of the week still mean something to a lot of people including Michelle because she's in the room we had to turn into a broadcasting studio for 3rd graders right now speaking in a different more professionally jubilant voice than the one I recognize as hers but for me and for a lot of people what does it mean anymore to be one day or the other? The signifier remains but the signified has been demeaned.

"Friday" then. Ok. If you say so pal. I seem to recall Friday but I just cannot place it.

People are bored with the virus Trump said the other day and that pretty much sums up his administration's approach to this whole thing. Fuck it not my problem. Even after they all got it. People just want this all to be over with he said essentially and he's right about that but for different reasons.

"It will go away," Trump said at the final debate. "We're rounding the turn, we're rounding the corner, it's going away."

There have been around a thousand new deaths a day this week and something like 70,000 new cases a day for a while now and people say it's a second wave but it doesn't feel like that it feels like the first one is still cresting although I don't know if it's accurate to refer to these clusters of death as waves anymore it's more like it's just the tide moving in and out.

THIS BOOK SHOULDN'T EXIST

This book shouldn't exist. That's not just a free burn for any critics who may end up reviewing it it's also a matter of fact. None of the events contained herein should have happened. As I'm writing at the end of August we're nearing 190,000 deaths from the coronavirus in the U.S. with over six million confirmed cases meaning people who will suffer as of yet unknown complications for months or for the rest of their lives. Meanwhile our peer countries around the world seem to have largely curtailed the spread of the virus for now and others including ones that many here look down upon when we tell ourselves the lies about American exceptionalism barely had any widespread death to speak of in the first place. "Barely any widespread death" throughout a country seems like a weird compliment but you know what I mean. It didn't have to be this way. It is but it didn't have to.

Six months into the pandemic the wearing of masks to help curtail the spread of the disease continues to be a partisan issue with videos emerging on social media every day of people absolutely losing their minds in grocery stores and restaurants when it is politely suggested that perhaps they might suffer through a few minutes of moderate inconvenience in order to potentially save the lives of their neighbors. We have always had to put a piece of fabric on our feet and ass and tits to go out in public or to a store but having to put a piece of fabric on our face now is tyranny for some reason.

All the while Donald Trump continues his assault on the looming election explicitly stating that he plans to neuter the Postal Service among other things because he suspects it will help his chances. There is no more quiet-part-loud it's all cacophony. Mail boxes are being removed in cities around the country as we speak and mail sorting machines are being mysteriously and coincidentally tossed into dumpsters. At least that is what we're worried about this week. There will have been a dozen other crises by the time you read this each dumber and scarier than the last.

In those same cities from Portland to Kenosha Black Lives Matter protesters continue to be brutalized by a violent unchecked mob of vicious thugs in uniform who've committed untold numbers of assaults and shootings on citizens who've gathered together to ask if maybe we could have a little bit less state-sanctioned murder in this country. The more we ask them to stop the more they seem to relish doing it out of spite. The beatings will continue until morale declines. And now the right have taken it upon themselves to act as deputies in a sort of auxiliary police force all with the full blessing of the president and his enablers. The tyrants the second amendment supporters have been preparing themselves for all these years have finally arrived and surprise! It's me and you not the actual oppressive government.

As the fall approaches politicians including Trump and the "good" governors are insisting in a lot of states that schools should reopen as normal. This despite the fact that many of them that have recently started in the late summer have announced widespread cases of community infection almost the instant they unlocked the doors.

"Teachers returned to a Georgia school district last week," a *Washington Post* headline I just saw read. "260 employees have already gone home to quarantine."

Imagine the first day of school on the morning announcements reading off the list of the newly dead.

Never mind that millions and millions of parents being forced to send their children back into the meat grinder are out of work which in America means they are shit out of luck when it comes to keeping their health insurance. As of this late date Joe Biden our presumptive savior from Donald Trump the first bad president has still not come out in favor of Medicare for All. In fact his pick for Vice President Kamala Harris reversed her previously stated support for the idea in order to play ball with the corporate Democrats.

Mercifully and only through sheer luck we have not as of yet been personally crushed by the violence of the pandemic only the psychological menace of it but it's looking like my wife Michelle will have to go back to teaching in a couple weeks against her wishes and the wishes of her union and all her colleagues. I have asked her not to do that to perhaps take a leave of absence or quit but if she does we'll have no health insurance and then what? In the midst of all this chaos we uprooted and moved outside of the Boston area for the first time in twenty years to a weird little suburb I've never even heard of and we are currently two mortgage payments into thirty years of debt which feels overwhelming at a time like this especially when the newspapers and websites around the country I might normally be employed by continue to be pillaged and sold off for spare parts by money ghouls with Fireball flowing where their blood should be.

Our move happened as brief eviction moratoriums in some states around the country are set to end and while 23 million are reportedly at risk of losing their homes according to the AP and 32% of Americans had outstanding housing payments at the beginning of August according to CNBC and while almost 30 million Americans reported not having enough to eat in the last week according to Bloomberg and the Senate has just recently gone on vacation for the rest of the summer. They passed no additional coronavirus relief package. We certainly never saw any relief ourselves did you?

I guess we're among the lucky ones but this stasis doesn't feel much like victory. And with the move came a sense of survivor's guilt as if we made it onto one of the escape pods just as the mothership exploded. What a weird feeling to suddenly have to mow a lawn for the first time since I was a child just as all my friends back in the city were confined to their small apartments. Not that the lawn in question isn't comically tiny mind you not to mention the house itself is actually smaller than our old apartment but there is more green space out here and fewer people in the streets and therefore we have added an extra layer of protection from the death in our neighbors' mouths.

I don't know what we're doing here man. I mean me writing this and the country at large. We're dying and starving and being beaten in the streets and the president is busy trying to make sure water pressure in showerheads is deregulated.

There will be a million books written about this period in history but most of them will come when it's all said and done. Writing about it now at the beginning of the pandemic—and to be clear we are still in the beginning of this in America despite being six months along—feels strange it feels like you've just jumped off a cliff into the ocean and as you're falling someone shouts out How's the water? and you yell back What? and then you keep falling.

I thought for some reason anyway I'd get a lot of this down as it was happening. Not for history because I hate that framing the idea that you hear so often now like "History won't look favorably on this" usually when it's someone panicking about Trump's latest fuck up. It's just such a strange way of thinking about the world to me. It's a form of punting responsibility for real problems happening right now to some later date at which point the future moon historians or whatever will arrive and right the wrongs of our present with their scathing appraisal of how terrible Trump was.

Not only is it a type of cowardice—"outsourcing this to the future when people will care" as a buddy of mine said—it doesn't even happen to be true. The history books do not in fact tell us the real unvarnished dirt on what our leaders and so on were up to that's like the one main thing we know about history books that they're fucked up and biased and written from the perspective of the victors. On top of that thinking about this particular pandemic in terms of what will be said about it later is just real fucking weird because did we even learn about the Spanish flu in the books we were meant to have read? I certainly don't remember reading about it in school.

I just read something H. L. Mencken wrote in 1956 about it.

"The influenza epidemic of 1919, though it had an enormous mortality in the United States and was, in fact, the worst epidemic since the Middle Ages, is seldom mentioned, and most Americans have apparently forgotten it. This is not surprising. The human mind always tries to expunge the intolerable from memory, just as it tries to conceal it while current."

I imagine we're similarly going to forget a lot of this so maybe this is just so I and maybe you remember what it felt like. What a luxury to still have memories.

The deal here will be familiar to anyone who read my last book or subscribes to the newsletter. It's me trying my best to share the stories of people being fucked in this house of horrors all while losing what's barely left of my mind in the process. The difference is this time that outside of a dozen or so marches and protests and vigils it's all been done from the comfort (?) of my own home. As it turns out it's a lot harder to write when you can't actually go anywhere to report on anything without risking your health and your scenery remains perfectly fixed and the total expanse of your universe is from that room over there to this room over here and sometimes down the street if you're lucky.

I may have been too hasty when I named my newsletter and last book *Welcome to Hell World*. What's the level below that called?

I WANT TO SWALLOW ALL THE DAYS AHEAD AT ONCE

It's March and I am a child who knows nothing and you are a child who knows nothing except that we can feel something moving in the basement and we know not to go down there. It's August and we're huddled in a besieged grocery store as terrific insects hurl themselves against the glass wearing the faces of our loved ones bearing invitations to playdates and barbecues.

It's March and I am a child who knows nothing and the idea of being isolated at home and unable to see anyone for weeks more never mind months more seems so suffocating that if I let myself envision it I feel like I'm going to collapse. Instead what I try to do is think about it one day at a time as the folks in the famous secret program which I probably will need to join after this is all over like to say. You don't have to survive and wait out the entirety of this thing all at once right now all you have to do is make it through today I told people back then when I was a child. Tomorrow will probably be the same shit and the day after that too but tomorrow isn't your problem at the moment I said but children like me are very famously idiots.

It's April and we've just moved into our new home and after over a month of quarantine I don't know if I can take

my own advice from way back in March anymore. I want
to swallow all the days ahead at once right now in one disgusting gulp like I'm trying to hide evidence from the police
or like I'm trying to smuggle the duration of the virus onto
an airplane and then I take a restless nap on the plane and
shit it out after and hand it off to someone else so it's not my
problem anymore. The relief when it's no longer in your pos-
session. I want to come out the other side. I want to get to the
part where we're all like What the fuck was that all about?
then we all go get egg sausage and cheese on an English muf-
fin at Dunkin' and eat it silently and very fast in a bustling
unworried crowd of people whose eyes don't have poison
inside of them.

It's August and I don't particularly care what happens
anymore or about the passage of time in general. Soon
Michelle will be forced into returning to school to teach a
roomful of children how not to die instead of how to do mul-
tiplication but no one in charge has of yet provided her with
that particular curriculum.

It's April and a reader writes to me about his time at war.

"I take the quarantine day by day and don't focus on the
end date, which is exactly how it was on my deployments to
Iraq. Once you get used to the kind of weird new part of life
of being shelled and fired at you fall into a routine of absolute monotony. Every day you trudge to the chow hall for
breakfast, trudge to work, trudge back to the chow hall for
lunch, trudge to work or work-related activity or meeting. Go
to the gym and spend at least two hours there just to waste
time. Everyone tells you not to keep track of the days or count

them down or whatever, but by the halfway mark everyone eventually ends up making one of these pie charts from a Microsoft Office program that tells you how much time you have left until you return home or return to normal."

I wonder if being shelled at would be worth it to be able to go to the gym at this point.

"By the end you are so bored and so want to be done with what you are currently stuck in that it becomes a physical feeling. It's hard to explain but it actually felt like it was mentally fatiguing. I read dozens of books on each deployment but by the end of them I couldn't read anymore because my angst would build to the point that I could feel it in my chest and then my throat."

I've only finished one book during the entirety of quarantine thus far it was *The Ministry of Fear* by Graham Greene. I've started many more but finishing a book or finishing anything besides maybe a bottle is a problem for me now.

The book is set during the Blitz in London and people go about their normal daily lives as best as possible going to work at a cafe and having social gatherings and church raffles and so on as the bombs drop all around them. A siren goes off and they all hide or brace themselves for the impact and hope the bombs fall somewhere else distant somewhere where they won't get them and then they get up after the dust clears the next day and do it all over again once the names of the dead have been reported dutifully in the newspaper. The characters in the book and the characters in the actual war had no idea when the war would end but we do and that's called irony unless I'm mistaken. We have no idea about when our own thing here will end at this point maybe the people reading this do and that's irony too.

A dozen or more friends' parents are gone now but I've been absurdly fortunate to have suffered no close personal loss throughout all of this which is a miracle of sorts. My sister who is a nurse that works with the elderly contracted the virus early on and was sick and exhausted and rundown for a couple of weeks but seems to have recovered. We still don't fully understand what recovering means at this point though. My good friend's father died in New York City and he talked to me about the ghastly absurdity of the nurse placing a phone up to his ear because of course he and his brothers couldn't go and say goodbye in person. They got to listen to him breathe for a while. My friend said he wasn't sure if his father knew they were there on the line so they ended up talking amongst themselves about other random shit and I wonder if their father laying there in the bed perhaps aware he was going to die presently thought to himself Jesus Christ with this shit.

Probably he was just happy to hear his children's voices.

It's March and a nurse named Celia Yap Banago who had worked for forty years at Research Medical Center in Kansas City and had expressed concern about the lack of proper protective equipment at the facility died after treating a patient that was positive for COVID-19. She was planning on retiring that week.

"I just feel like things may have gone differently had we had the proper protective equipment that we needed to care for our patient that night," her colleague Charlene Carter told KCRU.

"No nurse, no health care worker, should have to put their lives, their health, and their safety at risk for the failure of hospitals and our elected leaders to provide the protection they need to safely care for patients," <u>said</u> Bonnie Castillo, Executive Director of National Nurses United.

A phlebotomist named Deborah Gatewood also died from the virus around that time not long before she herself was set to retire from Beaumont Hospital in Farmington Hills, Michigan.

Gatewood's daughter Kaila Corrothers said her mother brought herself to the hospital where she worked for over thirty years on four separate occasions throughout March but was denied a test each time and sent home on one occasion with cough medicine. Here take this I imagine they said. It's nothing. Take this nothing home with you.

Eventually she was admitted to another hospital where she died on April 20.

"This did not have to happen this way," Corrothers said.

It took twenty years for over 58,000 Americans to die during the Vietnam War. Millions of non-Americans were killed too but we rarely count those when we're doing comparisons like this because they don't matter as much right? In any case in just a few months we easily cruised by that wretched milestone of dead Americans. Aside from that there aren't too many parallels between the war and the pandemic save from how cheaply our leaders view human life and how they'll spare no expense to defeat even the faintest sniff of communism or socialism from catching on lest people start getting any ideas about how things could improve somewhat.

It's late April and a *New York Times* analysis of everything the president has said at his press conferences since March 9 the early critical period when we could have done something found that Trump had mentioned the toll the virus has taken on the country "only fleetingly."

"By far the most recurring utterances from Mr. Trump in the briefings are self-congratulations, roughly 600 of them, which are often predicated on exaggerations and falsehoods."

Trump has occasionally attempted to display empathy throughout this which is notable in the way that watching a chimp in a hat and vest smoke a pack of cigarettes is notable but more often than not he's been focused on the harm done to his own reputation and the bank accounts of his rich donors.

It just occurs to me I have no idea how Iraq has been handling the pandemic or Vietnam for that matter. Around 4,500 deaths toward the end of July for the former which doesn't seem so bad especially when compared to how many Iraqis we killed for even stupider reasons and wait hold on this can't be right there have been no deaths from the virus in Vietnam?

It also occurred to me I have no idea what number we've got up on the big board here at home. I tried to Google it and I came across a *Washington Post* piece memorializing some of the dead including a young girl from Baltimore.

"Dar'Yana Dyson, 15, loved music and dancing, and dreamed of someday becoming a cosmetologist," it said. "The oldest of four children, she had a wry sense of humor, pranking her siblings even as she was being treated in the hospital. She was handy with technology, too, fixing the family's PlayStation and often posting videos from her cell phone. Perhaps most of all, she was known for her big, forgiving heart. 'You could make her mad,' her mother said, 'and she would see the good in you.'"

I can't find the number of deaths for some reason. I've misplaced the dead. I suppose it doesn't matter whatever it is today it will be vastly different by the time I turn this book in and greater still by the time this reaches you. I could be dead by then. You could be dead by then. I don't particularly want either of those things to come true although there are a few people I hope inside my heart won't make it through this every night when I lie down to forget about the carnivorous moths papering the windows and the grinning spider with grandma's face in the corner beckoning the children to sit on her lap because she misses them ever so much.

Oh hold on I just found the number we just passed 150,000 dead in America as of the writing of this chapter. Just another war we've lost in a long list of them. On the plus side I guess we finally figured out a way to stop school shootings. Or pause them anyway.

DEATH IS THE CAPITAL OF URUGUAY

On January 1, 2020 the first normal day of the last normal year 177 people were killed by guns in America including people who used the gun on themselves. That's almost twice as many that are killed on the average day in a typical year in our exceptionally average and typical country but by and large those deaths and the ones on the following day and the following day and the following day were invisible to most of us. No one cares about traffic in a city they don't live in. Two days after that we assassinated Qasem Soleimani the Iranian general and I remember being worried that untold numbers of people were about to die in the coming months and I was right about that just for the wrong reasons.

"I think it is entirely possible that this is going to be a catalyst inside Iran where the people celebrate this killing of Soleimani" Ari Fleischer said on Fox News that night and then Mike Pompeo went on and said "We have every expectation that people not only in Iraq, but in Iran, will view the American action last night as giving them freedom" and it occurred to me that the way we talk about the bombing violence we export to other countries is similar to the way we talk about the gun violence that we insist upon inflicting upon our own country in that in both cases it always comes framed in terms of extending freedoms and I suppose that's true in the sense that a bullet and a bomb do provide their target with a kind of freedom.

Refusing to wear a mask during a pandemic is a kind of freedom too.

On March 11, 2020 my last normal day I went to tell my therapist I wasn't going to see her anymore because I was moving soon and it felt like it was this big thing in my life like this momentous occasion and I felt conflicted and guilty about it like I was abandoning her and she said surprise motherfucker I was about to tell you I'm leaving too and we both said haha and then I went home and didn't leave for weeks. No that's a lie before I went home I went to the YMCA one last time for a swim and I had the pool almost entirely to myself which is a kind of luxury although how much pool can one person use. Liquids will take the shape of their container and gases will expand in volume to fill their container but a person stays the same size until they die and then they become very small.

I paused to take a break in the shallow end by the giant window overlooking the square outside and it was quiet save for the occasional siren from the nearby fire station and although the sun was shining it felt like everything was blanketed in snow. At this point I was still behaving normally in a world that wasn't which is honestly quite a reversal based on how things typically go in my brain. I asked the lifeguard if she thought it was safe to be in here and she said yes they were taking every precaution and I felt better because we want to be told things are fine by authorities even if the authority in question is just a college kid whose entire enforcement apparatus amounts to a whistle. I thought about how annoyed I would usually get when they would kick us out when a lightning storm was coming through but lightning is different than a virus I guess because you can at least see it for an instant.

In that last visit my therapist encouraged me once again to try to find something productive to do with my time besides drinking and going to the gym and looking at the news all day and I said I would but I was lying except for the stop going to the gym part because that decision was made for me and without my input almost immediately after by the famous mouth poison. I said I had been sleeping very poorly and she said I should look into getting more tryptophan in my diet you know like the stuff in turkey that makes you sleepy on Thanksgiving she said and I said I have heard of it. Apparently it can also improve your mood she said and I said that's crazy. Apparently there's a lot of it in pumpkin seeds too she said. Then I told her about a poem I had read called We Lived Happily During the War by Ilya Kaminsky and she hadn't heard of it but she never had heard of anything I referenced. I said I thought the things everyone else does when they read that particular poem such as wow and holy shit and then after a few minutes of sitting there with my mouth open after putting it down I thought like everyone else does after reading any particular poem fuck it fuck a poem it doesn't matter the poets have been trying to get us to see how terrible war and unnecessary death is since the invention of both poetry and death and it never works. The poets have lost that one in a rather lopsided defeat I am sad to report.

The thing about my therapist leaving was that she was going to start transitioning into remote therapy even before the virus she said and I have to say that was a pretty prescient decision on her part. Perhaps I should have listened to her more intently all this time about everything else. I asked her if she thought I had gotten any better since she first started seeing me a few years ago and she said I was a hard one to figure out and that I had definitely taken a lot of steps forward but then I often take two steps back so it's progress of a kind but not. After one good week of doing better I always think welp I'm cured baby time to get back to doing whatever the fuck I want and that's not a responsible way to manage anything whether it's your mental health or a country under a pandemic.

I said it was kind of hard to think about anything else at a time like this when we're waiting to find out how many people are going to die so most nights what I do is I say fuck it I'm going to drink a gallon of alcohol and then I do so even though I don't really want to. Self-medicating is very good it's like punting on first down every time you get the ball and occasionally running 70 yards the wrong way for a safety. I said it feels like it felt when I thought we were going to go to war earlier in the year like a creeping and overwhelming sense of existential dread but it was tempered with a sense of something like stolen valor because while I didn't know who they were or how many people would be killed throughout all this I was fairly certain I was not going to number among them and so the despair felt unearned. Everyone knows they are going to die but it is also an impossibility to hold on to for more than a moment it's like looking directly into the sun.

Death is a fact but it's easy to forget and there are lots of things like that right where you know them to be true but you don't know them know them like someone could ask you what the capital of Uruguay is and you'd go shit shit hold on then they'd say Montevideo and you'd go I knew that. And you did know it too you just couldn't access it. Death is the capital of Uruguay is the point.

Ok maybe it happened like this. On the last normal day I was wrenched out of sleep like a fish on a hook and I clambered out of bed and I slipped on the old shoes I keep by the door and I went outside to the porch and I sat there shivering in the cold watching the long tail of a plane graffiti the sky white and it looked like it was heading straight downward at a ninety degree angle and I thought holy shit it's plummeting! but no it was just a trick of perspective and eventually it disappeared and went wherever it is planes go. For a couple of minutes those people's lives were my problem and then they weren't. Now they'll just go on to live for a while and then die in some other way I won't ever have to know about like pretty much everyone else ever.

The last time I was on a plane was in January to go to New York to do my *Hell World* book reading at The Strand and so many people came I thought this is going to be my year man. Things are about to happen. Sometimes I try to outsmart the system by flying to New York instead of taking the train but you can't fix it it takes four or five hours to get to New York no matter how you try to get around it. I won't be going back to New York any time in the foreseeable future and that makes me sad but on the other hand think of the money I'll save!

I drove to Dunkin' Donuts for what would be the last time in a couple months that plane morning with a frosted windshield I couldn't get to clear up so I had to keep firing the wiper fluid which would work for a second and then it would freeze almost instantly and I basically kept having to do that for five minutes until I got there. I thought about dying in a plane crash and so naturally I thought about a song by Albert Hammond who I had weirdly gotten really into around then and it went like "And I don't wanna die for no good reason. I just wanna go on and on."

I just saw a while ago there was some sort of online tribute to Joe Strummer due to it was his birthday and that dude's son Albert Hammond Jr. was going to perform I guess and I realized one way to get people to remember you when you die is to write something as good as London Calling so maybe I should try something like that how hard can it be.

On the way back from Dunkins I had to stop in the middle of the road because there was a family of turkeys which I guess is called a "rafter" crossing and I stopped because of course I didn't want to kill them and that seemed strange because I must have caused the death of so many turkeys in my life. I guess the difference is it's only acceptable to me when turkeys are killed by the millions when someone else is doing it and I don't have to be there while it happens.

I just read an article that said maybe the reason a lot of people seem to generally not give much of a fuck about the over 200,000 Americans that have died from the virus in the past seven months is because we've been so successfully conditioned to ignore the deaths caused by our endless wars around the globe. Remember how it was a whole thing when George Bush made it so we couldn't look at the coffins coming back from the Middle East?

They say that infants develop object permanence by about the age of two meaning that they come to understand that objects and people continue to have a separate and permanent existence even when they're outside the bounds of their immediate sensory experience but I don't know that we necessarily always hold onto that ability when we get older. Sometimes I look at my wife sitting over there on the couch eating cereal like she is right now and I remember that she is an entirely separate entity with her own internal life and all her own fucking things going on.

Something I think about a lot and I'm not projecting this will be the time is the idea of the final joke. Like we'll all obviously joke online through almost everything no matter how bad but someday there might be a thing where we don't want to anymore. Whatever the last joke is going to be it won't be funny.

On my last normal night before they started running the death toll odometer on the TV regularly Sarah Palin appeared on the show The Masked Singer and performed "Baby Got Back" by Sir Mix-a-Lot in a pink bear costume. "This is the weirdest thing I've ever done, that's for sure," she said. "But it's all about fun. It's unity. This is all good. This is something that our country needs right now, too." And then immediately after it ended president Donald Trump came on the TV to reassure the country about our approach to the virus and fucked up like three things instantly that his people had to walk back. You could actually feel the strangeness of the programming transition as it happened and I don't think I could write anything in here that more accurately summarizes the place we are in in 2020 except for maybe this next thing.

I just saw an extraordinary photograph taken by Noah Berger for the Associated Press of a sign outside of a building in California. Senior Center the top of the sign says. Come Join Us the bottom says and then in the middle it reads Wear a Mask Wash Your Hands Social Distance Stay Safe and all around it the entire local world is engulfed in flames because California is currently on fire like it often simply just is. And then I read that there aren't enough people to fight the wildfires in the state right now because they usually use prison labor for that particular task and so many of them aren't available because they're on lockdown sick with the virus due to the governor there and governors everywhere else pretty much left them to die.

In my last normal week some random food magazine asked me if I wanted to write about the history of lemonade stands in America and I was like uh then they said they'd pay me a good sum and I said can I be political and they said ok and so I said ok and so I was doing my little research and writing my cute little jokes and japes and so on and the line I wanted to draw was from how the lemonade stand is this iconic American thing that is supposed to teach children about running a business and the glories of capitalism and so on and I wanted to get up to the era we're in now where kids are starting lemonade stands to help pay off their classmates' school lunch debt and their mommies' cancer bills and then I randomly came across a picture someone had posted of a young boy and his friends and they were selling toilet paper for $2 a roll at a little stand with a sign and everything and it said Don't get left behind next to the emoji of a smiling piece of shit and the whole overarching metaphor for the piece and everything else for that matter basically wrote itself.

About thirteen years ago when we were first moving into the apartment we finally left in April in the middle of a pandemic I was having trouble getting the mattress and box-spring up the narrow stairs so I rigged some sort of half-assed rope system by which I was going to hoist them up over the second story back porch and get them in that way and I was struggling with it it was just me and Michelle and her mother and I guess it probably looked like I was going to fly off the side of the porch to my certain doom and the neighbor next door the retired veteran who hates Trump and loves the Red Sox but also hates them sprang into action and came over and saved the day. Sometimes I still think about being launched off the side of the porch like being tossed in a tre-buchet and I wonder if I landed on the mattress just so if I would've been alright.

I was thinking about that because just around my last normal day we found a house to move into in the suburbs and I spent those finals weeks of normalcy trying to throw out all the shit I'd accumulated over the years week by week and I started to get really nervous about contending with the fucking mattress again because I am far weaker and a lot less fearless than I was back then. I get weaker and less fearless every single day and I guess it just goes on like that forever.

The thing I did when it came to going through my old shit and deciding what to throw away or not was to make like Orpheus and just don't look back. You can't look back or the spell will be broken. Throw it all away. Every day of that last week I'd pack up a box of things that were once important to me until they were not and deliver them to the Goodwill store until they closed due to the sickness and whatever was left I guess I was meant to keep forever so I did.

All of your weird methods of blocking out the sun have been terrible Michelle told me after we got the curtains set up here in our new home. We were talking about the various shitty apartments we've lived in over the years. The last one we moved into when I was twenty-eight which is a child's age. I wonder what I thought about back then I said. I have no idea. I have no idea what sorts of things were going through my mind that long ago. She said when she first met me I had curtains duct taped over the windows and I gather I was either too poor or too stupid to figure out how curtain rods worked at the time.

Somewhere in the middle of all this in the middle of the new normal I posted four photos to Instagram from the last couple weeks before the thing started and captioned them the last time I had hope the last time I had fun the last time I went on a date with Michelle and the last time I jerked off in a doctor's office. I suppose the latter two are self-explanatory.

We went to our favorite local pub in the town we don't live in anymore and in the photo she's smiling real big in the way she does and I am making a gross face in the way I do and we had no idea that we would never go there or pretty much anywhere we liked to go ever again before leaving the area. I would have appreciated it more had I known at the time. I would have appreciated a lot of people and things a lot more had I known I was about to lose them.

In the doctor's office I was trying to find out if it was too late for me to bring a child into the world at this point in my life and I guess it technically isn't via what happened when the cum doctor looked at my cum under the microscope and said it's perfectly normal cum but I don't know if this is the type of world or country I can feasibly wrench a soul out of the void and drag them into. Sometimes I feel bad if I invite someone to like a party or a show and they don't end up having a good time so I can't imagine what it feels like to do that to someone only it's everything they ever have to do and experience in their entire life however long it might last. Sorry! Hope you had a nice time.

The last time I had fun was a picture of me at the end of February in the middle of a crowd at Emo Night Boston the monthly party I host and DJ with my friends and I've got both my hands raised in the air and this look on my face I don't recognize in myself which I gather must be joy and everyone around me is dancing and singing and sweating and spitting and spilling beer on each other and they're frozen still in time in the midst of it all now with no idea that it was probably the last time we'd do anything like that for the foreseeable future.

The last time I had hope was right around then too it was at the University of New Hampshire and Michelle and I had driven up there for a Bernie Sanders rally headlined by The Strokes one of our favorite bands in the world. When we got there the line was so long outside and it was so cold the type of cold where you draft off of strangers' body heat and use them to hide from the wind and don't think twice about it. Inside the lineup of electrifying speakers like Cornel West and AOC and Bernie himself and Nina Turner explained to a crowd of around 7,000 people in no uncertain terms that a better country was in fact possible and that we were this close to getting there.

Turner asked us all to raise one hand for ourselves so I did and we all did. Then raise another hand for someone else she said and she asked us to fight for someone we don't know as hard as we would for ourselves and for a couple weeks there when things were still normal I actually thought that enough of us in this country meant it but I was stupid to think that.

Later on in the night The Strokes played "New York City Cops" and everyone crashed the stage and it seemed like the beginning of a new era and it was just not in the way I thought it was going to be and then we walked back to the car along the slick hilly iced-over streets of Durham taking the tiniest possible steps hoping we wouldn't slip and break something because if we got hurt we might not be able to afford the medical bills and I wondered what it might be like to not have to worry about things like that anymore and I thought something is going to change man and it was about to indeed just not in the way I thought it was.

Somewhere along the way on the ride home we got a call that the bid we had put in on the house we live in now went through and Michelle was so happy and I was so mad because I didn't ever really believe I was actually going to become a homeowner in the suburbs and apparently I did a very bad job of hiding my disappointment. All of the things I was never going to be able to do again spread out before me in a temporal cartography of loss. All the concerts I wouldn't go to now that they're much further away to get to and all the friends I wouldn't visit and all the restaurants and bars in the city I would probably not get around to checking out and I saw my entire life getting smaller and the expanse of where I could go shrink and we had a bad fight about it but the joke was on me because all that shit disappeared for everyone and now everywhere is the suburbs and there's nowhere to go no matter where you live. It's a kind of death in a way like Montevideo but we're mercifully still alive just not in the way we thought we were going to be.

EVERY DAY I LEARN OF A NEW HORROR OF THE AMERICAN HEALTHCARE SYSTEM

It's March and it's sunny and quiet in my old neighborhood. Too quiet except for the birds. It feels like there's a blizzard outside that you can't see.

Toward the end of February which is the first time as best I can tell I personally acknowledged the existence of the coronavirus I sent out a tweet that went viral: "I like how the experts on TV say if you think you have coronavirus call your doctor ok lol let me just get my doctor on the phone the thing you can do."

Around fifty million Americans have donated to a crowd-funding campaign for medical bills or treatment <u>according to a survey</u> by the National Opinion Research Center at the University of Chicago. This may or may not be related to any problems we're experiencing at the moment in July as 5.4 million people have lost their job-provided health care insurance last I checked.

The survey also found that "an estimated eight million Americans had started a campaign for themselves or someone in their household and more than twelve million Americans had started a campaign for someone else."

"Although more people gained insurance coverage with the Affordable Care Act," they wrote, "crowdfunding for health care expenses is becoming more common because Americans still cannot afford their out-of-pocket costs—deductibles, copays, or coinsurance—their coverage notwithstanding. Medical bills remain the number one reason Americans file for personal bankruptcy, according to a 2019 City University of New York-Harvard study. When asked who is responsible for paying for care for those who cannot afford it, a majority of Americans (60 percent) believe the government should as opposed to health care providers, charities, and family and friends."

In late July the Democrats' platform committee voted against including support for Medicare for All.

I'm so fucking sick of being told people like me and presumably you if you are reading this book are too angry about healthcare. If anything we aren't yet angry enough.

A recent study from Yale researchers says we'll actually save money—and lives—under Medicare for All.

"Although health care expenditure per capita is higher in the USA than in any other country, more than 37 million Americans do not have health insurance, and 41 million more have inadequate access to care," they write. "By contrast, a universal system, such as that proposed in the Medicare for All Act, has the potential to transform the availability and efficiency of American health-care services."

Not only would it literally cost less than what we pay now but "ensuring health-care access for all Americans would save more than 68,000 lives and 1.73 million life-years every year compared with the status quo."

Just as the pandemic was kicking off I spoke with a former nurse who worked for years in Texas and California because she genuinely wanted to help people. What she found instead was an insurance bureaucracy dedicated to extracting wealth from the bodies of the injured and the sick and even more exasperating for her doctors who were willing to manipulate that system to enrich themselves. After working for a particularly malicious surgeon she decided she could no longer in good conscience be a part of that system.

"Nurses are truly nurturers," she told me. "I don't think we would be nurses if we weren't, but the healthcare industry does something to you. It's become a black void of greed and corporate shills who have no regards for the sanctity of life. I could no longer do a job I loved because I believe in compassion, selflessness, and solidarity with my fellow humans, you know?"

"I've told a patient who had just been diagnosed with terminal lung cancer that their insurance company would not pay for treatment because they themselves were not deemed viable," she told me. "I've told women with breast cancer their insurance has denied a second mammogram for being medically unnecessary. I've told parents who were barely hanging on to hope that their insurance was not in-network so we would be sending their child six hours away to another, less qualified facility."

Despite personally living a life that could be destroyed instantly with a bad healthcare break like most of you I also live the relative life of a king compared to millions in this country. It's simply unjust and it disgusts me that people doing ok like me seem to care more about the millions being crushed today as we speak than the people who are doing very well like all of the rich cable news personalities and untouched Democrats who think better healthcare is akin to installing a Communist dictatorship. Not only before the pandemic they still think that right now!

Dealing with the right is one thing but it's real fucking grim and demoralizing having to contend with so many "on the left" who don't think better things are possible and don't seem to even want to try. I get that coming from the rich TV people they have their own class interests to protect but I don't understand the average person who goes to bat for the status quo.

The thing that bothers me the most just as the pandemic has made evident the evils of our current system is this: You can literally just say you want the best and most just outcome for whatever issue at any time. A lot of people don't seem to get that. It's free! You do not as an individual have a limited reserve of justice aspiration coupons to redeem. You're not managing a fantasy football team or whatever where you can only draft one tight end. You can ask for the fucking moon or you can simply ask that our country accept a little bit more social democracy. You don't have to think Well how will we pay for it? you don't have to think Hmm will the other side be mad at me for wanting this? you don't have to think about what the voters of a lawmaker in a purple state might want you can just say THIS IS FUCKING CRAZY AND WE NEED

TO MAKE THINGS BETTER. You can say it ten thousand times in a row. And then when enough of us are saying it the politicians will have to listen or it's their ass.

Countless hours of watching cable news pundits has convinced the average person they have to think like a savvy politics insider who knows how the game is played and that always means hamstringing our aspirations for progress before we even get to the bargaining table. You don't have to do that shit man. It's not your job to worry about that shit. You don't have to see Chuck and Nancy caving in to the Republicans' demands on unemployment insurance in the middle of a historic devastating plague with millions out of work and millions infected and say ah well they are doing their best.

The only conclusion I can draw from people who aren't demanding that things can and should be better is that they don't particularly care if things get better or not because things are already fine enough for them.

But maybe there are other ways to improve healthcare (or whatever) people will say maybe we just need to go a little slower and not make such radical leaps all at once they say and to them I say "more likely to work" and reasonable process arguments are always always always a way of forestalling progress. It's a condescending appeal to fake reasonability and a lie that says we'll get to your shit eventually just hold on and to that I say no go fuck your mother. It's also how we end up with a mostly invisible candidate in the form of Joe Biden at a time when we are uniquely situated for real change.

I've said this before but as a reminder all of you fucking worms who aren't all in on eliminating the predatory health insurance industry today are going to lie and pretend you were all along at some point when retrospect makes it seem insane.

Whether it's climate change or healthcare or the pandemic or any of the other dozens of crises we're facing there are always going to be people who are paid very well to tell you that we just have to chill out and let progress wind its slow meandering course. They'll say it's too expensive or that the rules must be followed and the choice we have is whether to stand there over a dying man's body afraid to do anything to help because it might cost too much of a rich person's money to do so or to fucking take what we want because it's already ours.

Ok wait I lied the first time I tweeted about the virus was the day before the doctor one. I said this: "I will never contract nor die from the famous virus COVID-19 better known colloquially as the coronavirus." Back then it seemed ok to joke about.

Shortly before that Alex Azar the U.S. Secretary of Health and Human Services and a former pharmaceutical lobbyist and the vice president of Eli Lilly & Co. was at a hearing refusing to commit to Congress that any vaccine eventually developed for the virus would be made affordable for all Americans. "We would want to ensure that we work to make it affordable," he said. "But we can't control that price because we need the private sector to invest."

After the tweet about calling your doctor took off dozens of readers wrote in to me to confirm the absurdity of it. Here is a small sampling of what they said.

- I don't have a doctor. I have an urgent care clinic I can sit in for five hours coughing till I see a nurse practitioner who tells me to go home and drink fluids.
- I haven't had a "my doctor" since I was last able to qualify under my mother's workplace insurance so that would be some fifteen plus years ago. Frankly the idea of having a doctor you regularly see is an alien concept at this point.
- If you can't get the doctor on the phone, just take a helicopter to your family's wing at the local hospital.
- This is why I just love it when people are like "we can't have Medicare for All because other countries have to wait forever to see a doctor!" I had to wait six months last time I wanted to see my PCP for insomnia and when I did her literal words were "I don't know. Try chamomile."
- For most of us it's "call your nurse line and get referred to an emergency room." Having a doctor you can call seems like a fucking myth.
- When I went into urgent care for bronchitis, the nurse practitioner told me "after you finish the round of antibiotics, follow up with your PCP." "You . . . *you* are my PCP."

- I've been to my doctor's office four times in the last year and have not seen my doctor. I think he might have died and the staff is covering it up.
- Laughing because I have never spoken to LET ALONE met my doctor. I have one and they just send me nurses when I make appts. This shit is COMICAL.

Back in February when I still had hope I went to a number of Bernie Sanders rallies and at one in New Hampshire I stood there with my hand raised like a nerd for a half hour because I wanted to ask him something along the lines of: When we all hear these stories about people's lives being crushed under the weight of the predatory for-profit healthcare industry in this country the very natural response at least for me is that that is fucked and we have to stop it. So many other people see it and think Eh that's not my problem. You cannot legislate empathy I wanted to say. So how at long last do we convince anyone to care about other people?

I never got a chance to ask though. No one else since then has come up with an answer.

NO CORNER OF THE NATION WILL BE LEFT UNTOUCHED

In every disaster or apocalypse movie there's always a character that is meant to be the stand in for capitalism who remains motivated by profit long after it seems reasonable. Everyone else by this point is panicking or fortifying things or dying or killing but this type of guy is still dreaming about the potential windfall at hand for the company or packing briefcases of cash or jewels or whatever instead of supplies and we all think look at this vile weenie and we hate him so much. In the movie the guy gets owned almost instantly after that and we all cheer but of course it doesn't work that way in real life.

I was thinking about this in March as I saw Rush Limbaugh downplaying the threat of the virus.

"Who cares if it's ten times more lethal than the flu?" he said. "What does lethal mean?"

Another thing about movies about the end of the world is we're always sort of skeptical that things could go to all hell as quickly as they do and you think ah come on the army or whoever would have gotten control of this by now wouldn't they but of course it doesn't work that way in real life. In fact at the end of July as I write this sentence the army or the troops or whatever branch of the secret police it is Trump is deploying around the country are currently doing their level best at making everything much worse by continuing to beat and shoot at citizens and whisking them away without charges and without identifying themselves or their agency. It's August now and I just watched a video of police I think (?) in New York City kidnap a protester off the street and toss her into an unmarked minivan.

It's June and I'm staring into the faces of a row of all different types of police lined up along the streets of Boston just waiting for the slightest excuse to beat the shit out of me and my friends. The tension of it. They want it so badly.

I read a piece in the *New York Times* that said "As infections mount across the country, it is dawning on Americans that the epidemic is now unstoppable, and that no corner of the nation will be left untouched."

"In most states, contact tracing is now moot—there are simply too many cases to track. And while progress has been made on vaccines, none is expected to arrive this winter in time to stave off what many fear will be a new wave of deaths."

"Overall, the scientists conveyed a pervasive sense of sadness and exhaustion. Where once there was defiance, and then a growing sense of dread, now there seems to be sorrow and frustration, a feeling that so many funerals never had to happen and that nothing is going well. The United States is a wounded giant, while much of Europe, which was hit first, is recovering and reopening—although not to us."

I imagine you've often dreamed about leaving the country someday if things ever got bad enough but now here we are and they're so bad no one will even take us.

"We're all incredibly depressed and in shock at how out of control the virus is in the U.S.," said Dr. Michele Barry, the director of the Center for Innovation in Global Health at Stanford University.

"With so much wealth and medical talent, they asked, how could we have done so poorly? How did we fare not just worse than autocratic China and isolated New Zealand, but also worse than tiny, much poorer nations like Vietnam and Rwanda?"

It's March and I went outside at 6:30 am to sit on the porch at the apartment I don't live in anymore in fact it's one of our last days here and I looked at the sky and it was a beautiful pink and orange not the most beautiful pink and orange I've ever seen but nice enough to look at for a minute anyway and then I heard someone yell my name and I looked down and it was my old neighbor the retired veteran who mercifully for our ability to talk about things hates the president's fucking guts too and he said something like the fucking guy finally started taking it seriously last night and I said he's been dragging his heels on it for a month and he said I know. I said it would be pretty funny if he got it and he was about to agree with me but he caught himself and he said well I don't wish death on him I'm a Catholic and I'm on my way to Mass and I said well you're a better person than me please pray for me and he said he would so I should be covered for a while anyway vis-à-vis the maintenance of my eternal soul.

A weird thing about being a scumbag addict or drinker is that it's hard to ever know if you're coming down with a cold or the flu or whatever because you just generally always feel this way. Probably not the healthiest manner to conduct oneself during a plague.

No one who has spent an hour watching Trump speak never mind listened to him say specifically out loud that he was trying to keep the number of reported cases of coronavirus down over the past couple of months has any doubt he deliberately sabotaged the response for his own gain because he seemed to think even admitting there was a problem in the first place would make him look bad. And yet all along the media had to tiptoe around this obvious fact.

If our media were able to speak the truth freely it would've said from day one that he is putting us all in danger but instead they all still think they have to talk to people on background and do sourced reporting to confirm what is blatantly fucking obvious every single time Trump pulls some shit like this. Still three and half years in we're doing this. Just watch the man speak on TV! Trump will go on TV five days in a row saying ah I don't like the number to be big I like it small and then reporters have to go make like twenty phone calls and shit to get an Official on background so they can report the truth everyone already knows.

Last night when I was sitting outside watching the sun go down too late to seem natural it was less quiet than it is now. It was one of those nights when you hear the fire and police blasting their trumpets by and you imagine a whole fucking thing transpiring instead of just ignoring it like usual. Every siren always represents a tragedy of one kind or another under normal circumstances but there's something about the feeling in the air now that it's coming for you you just don't know it yet.

Another thing that happens in zombie movies is there is always a guy who's like trying to save his obviously sick wife long after it's clear that she's done for and we all watch and say ah come on man because you know he's gonna fuck it up for everyone else and I was thinking about that yesterday and I had one of those bad day nightmares that your brain shoots off into sometimes like a parallel timeline opens up and you follow it and get shivers and you actually have to say no! to make your brain stop thinking it but anyway the point is I decided I would do that shit I would probably endanger the entire world if it meant saving my wife so I'm sorry in advance if it ever comes to that. I would drive my zombie wife to the hospital then she would bite my fucking neck and not in the good way.

HOW LONG DOES IT TAKE YOU TO REMEMBER?

It finally struck me after a few weeks that my life hasn't changed much. The ambient dread has increased a certain degree but that was always there. The disgust at the holes in our social safety net being exposed has increased a certain degree but that too was always there. Sitting inside letting the news wash over me in waves alternately dull and pummeling or sharp and piercing is something I'm accustomed to. A sort of heightened hopelessness jockeying with brief flashes of optimism is familiar to me. I can't go to the pool anymore to swim but I can plan my day around an afternoon run which is now my one reason to leave the house. Yesterday for about ten minutes in the middle of running I forgot about the world and it was the most peaceful ten minutes I've had in a long time. Then some booger teens playing grabass on the path bombed up behind me and I wanted to beat their asses but then I remembered about not getting too close.

How long does it take you to ~remember~ when you wake up by the way? Do any of you make it an entire minute? Michelle said she's good for about five to ten seconds of blissful ignorance per morning. This morning I was awoken by landscapers blasting leaf blowers in the neighborhood for what seemed like an hour and aside from being annoyed by it I thought maybe blowing shit around all over the place right now isn't a good idea?

In any case what I was trying to say up above is the general trajectory of each day for me now is a ramping up to the hour that I have deemed socially acceptable to pour myself a drink and that's pretty much what life has been for the past year or two anyway. Nothing else really matters after that.

I wonder if the addicts and the cripplingly depressed are better prepared for all this? We recently watched the Lars von Trier film *Melancholia* in which depression is a sort of super power at the end of the world. Or a shield anyway.

On the final day when the planet Melancholia is about to collide with Earth Kirsten Dunst's character Justine and her sister Charlotte Gainsbourg's Claire have swapped roles. Previously catatonic with depression Justine is calmer and Claire the capable no-nonsense woman is being driven insane by the now impossible to ignore end of life as we know it. I guess one idea at play is that for people with some kinds of depression the arrival of doom isn't always as shattering as it is for everyone else because they've been expecting it anyway? Maybe that's not a thing in real life.

I've been reading reviews of the film all morning and comments on the reviews and I just came across this one.

"I liked it in general—it still haunts me—but there is not one likable character in the entire film. Every single person is an unforgivable douchebag. At the end I was rather glad to see the earth destroyed."

I don't really think that at the moment right now by the way if it makes any difference to you what I think. I'd like to see the world and all of us avoid destruction very much.

It's fucked up to me that everyone who has fake jobs that contribute very little to the operation of our society like me all get to stay home and pontificate but the people with the real jobs like grocery clerks or garbage men are still out there doing them. Well not all of them Michelle has a real job as a teacher and she's sitting here freaking out like everyone else.

It's August now and sanitation workers in New Orleans have been on strike since May asking for the very reasonable demands of a little bit more money and better safety conditions but that is a bridge too far apparently.

"I have been that person," City Waste Union representative Daytrian Wilken said in an interview for the Hell World newsletter. "I would take everything out of my house I didn't want, I would put it in the trash, I would drag it out to the curb, and I had no knowledge of the person who took my trash out—what they went through, what they were facing, what they even look like. I think It just never dawned on me that even if it rains, the guys are out there, and even if it's hot as hell those guys [are] out there."

A reporter from Vice asked people how they're dealing with despair right now and I said some shit like this below.

"There's this real weird back and forth going on in my mind right now like, this is what I've been trying to say all along people! This is how broken our country is! And then to be proven right in one fell swoop about how cruel our system is? There's no solace in that. It's not like one can gloat or anything if that makes sense. And on top of that there is still so much idiotic partisan bickering going on as we speak. It's just real grim. For even the most cynical among us who know how stupid and unqualified our leaders are, you sort of still always have a reserve chamber of·optimism right? We all must or else how would we get out of bed in the morning? The feeling that, when the shit hits the fan, the proper fail-safes will hold and so on. But here we are. I can't even take joy in the lol look at how bad Trump is fucking up thing because the bill for all that is finally coming due."

Other than that I told him I've got real bad diarrhea all the time.

My wife and I keep tagging in and out like only one of us can be freaking out at a time so it's currently my turn as I'm writing here. Soon she'll start getting really anxious then I'll have to put my fear aside and become the calm one again and I guess it will just go back and forth like that until there's something that arrives in the form of good news.

I SIMPLY CANNOT DO THIS

It's March and it was reported that a seventeen-year-old boy in Los Angeles County had died from symptoms associated with the coronavirus. The boy went to an urgent care clinic with respiratory symptoms and was denied treatment there R. Rex Parris the mayor of Lancaster explained in a video.

"He didn't have insurance, so they did not treat him," the mayor said so the facility told him to try the emergency room at a local hospital. On the way there he went into cardiac arrest and he died a few hours later. But soon after health officials there weren't so sure that the coronavirus was actually technically the cause of his death so they took the points down off the board which is great news because he would've been the first teenager believed to have died from it. Instead now he's just a teenager who died because he couldn't get treatment due to not having health insurance. It's just regular Hell World shit not Hell World 2 and that is better for some reason I guess.

Back then we didn't think young people could die from it.

I would like to beg the news media to stop showing me what the stock market is doing no one knows or cares what the stock market is it's like being shown the heart rate of a small group of people on a distant roller coaster we've never been on and will never get to go on and it's like the main thing they talk about.

A thing that has been dawning on me is that my typical vibe of withdrawing from the world and into my depression felt subversive when everything else was going on as normal around me but when it's my only choice it feels a lot less appealing.

My editor here at OR Books highlighted for me this passage from Slavoj Žižek's latest book *Pandemic!* which they recently published and which he said reminded him of my thinking on the matter of enforced isolation. It is of course much better written and thought out than my effort because he is Žižek and I'm some dipshit Boston Celtics fan.

"Let me begin with a personal confession: I like the idea of being confined to one's apartment, with all the time needed to read and work. Even when I travel, I prefer to stay in a nice hotel room and ignore all the attractions of the place I'm visiting. A good essay on a famous painting means much more to me than seeing this painting in a crowded museum. But I've noticed this makes now being obliged to confine myself more difficult. To help explain this let me recount, not for the first time, the famous joke from Ernst Lubitsch's *Ninotchka*: "'Waiter! A cup of coffee without cream, please!'" "I'm sorry, sir, we have no cream, only milk, so can it be a coffee without milk?"' At the factual level, the coffee remains the same, what changes is making the coffee without cream into coffee without milk—or, more simply even, adding the implied negation and making the simple coffee into a coffee without milk. The same thing has happened to my isolation. Prior to the crisis, it was an isolation 'without milk'—I could have gone out, I just chose not to. Now it's just the plain coffee of isolation with no possible negation implied."

It's April now and it's July and it's 2021 and the one day at a time thing is wearing thin in terms of both the pandemic and trying not to drink myself into oblivion every night because at least when I do that I get to feel something different.

No no I still think maintaining hope is the best approach right now at this moment but there will come an hour or two every day now where I lose my grasp on that and think what is the point fuck this and fuck me and fuck everything I simply cannot do this. Then I'll remember I can. Then I'll forget again.

I don't know maybe that's all dog shit and dumb and harmful to think. I don't know anything and as I typically say please do not look to me as a model of behavior of any kind.

In any case watching this all unfold hasn't exactly been great for someone who already had a tenuous grasp on staying alive under normal circumstances. As my favorite piece of shit racist singer Morrissey once said "When I'm lying in my bed I think about life and I think about death and neither one particularly appeals to me."

Mostly my reasons for enjoying the not-drinking times was because I was sick of feeling tired all the time and being unproductive with work and gaining weight and being a real fucking asshole when I drink and all the usual shit but now that we've basically lived inside for months does any of that matter at the moment?

I don't know.

It does.

I think.

I don't know.

It's hard to think clearly right now since Michelle is having a video meeting with her third graders across the room. She told me to please try not to blast a huge fart in the middle of it and it's hard because my guts are fucked right now.

I don't know.

It's August now. How are you guys holding up? No seriously how are you? Not great I'm guessing based on recent findings from the CDC.

"Symptoms of anxiety disorder and depressive disorder increased considerably in the United States during April–June of 2020, compared with the same period in 2019," they report which sounds obvious but I suppose it's still helpful to see some data anyway.

"Overall, 40.9% of respondents reported at least one adverse mental or behavioral health condition, including symptoms of anxiety disorder or depressive disorder (30.9%), symptoms of a trauma- and stressor-related disorder related to the pandemic (26.3%), and having started or increased substance use to cope with stress or emotions related to COVID-19 (13.3%)," the report explains and that seems alarming sure but it also seems a little low right? Who are the people not experiencing any adverse mental or behavioral health conditions right now? Besides the untouched and unbothered rich I mean. What must that kind of life be like? To have made it this far into the pandemic without breaking down at least once or twice doesn't seem like evidence of a healthy functioning brain to me does it?

Maybe it's all the people partying in Vegas. ProPublica looked at cell phone data tracking people on the Vegas Strip during a four day period over a weekend in July identifying around 26,000 individuals.

"Some of those same smartphones also showed up in every state on the mainland except Maine in those same four days," they write.

"About 3,700 of the devices were spotted in Southern California in the same four days; about 2,700 in Arizona, with 740 in Phoenix; around 1,000 in Texas; more than 800 in Milwaukee, Detroit, Chicago and Cleveland; and more than 100 in the New York area."

"'The cellphone analysis highlights a reason the virus keeps spreading,' said Oscar Alleyne, an epidemiologist and chief program officer with the National Association of County and City Health Officials. 'People have been highly mobile, and as a result, it makes sense why we see the continuation of the surge.'"

Can you imagine being in Vegas right now or anywhere for that matter. Even under normal circumstances it's a loathsome middle-finger-to-god of a city that shouldn't exist. I have nonetheless had a couple of great times there!

To be clear our utter failure to deal with this pandemic in any serious way does not come down to individuals making bad choices it's more to do with the incompetence and often malevolence of our leaders who've done the bare minimum possible all along the way when it comes to installing comprehensive and consistent public health policies like many other countries with death in the rearview did early on but at the same I don't know maybe don't travel to Vegas right now? Or anywhere? It's like how they tried to convince people the blame for ruining the environment was on us for making irresponsible consumption choices and not on the like ten massive multinational polluters who run the poison factories around the world. Even still that doesn't give us carte blanche to bury our used hypodermic needles in the sand at the beach or to save up our six-pack rings to go dump into the nearest dolphin sanctuary.

Not that this massive humiliating and devastating wave of unnecessary death won't stop those same negligent leaders from taking victory laps. Andrew Cuomo who oversaw over 32,000 deaths in his state alone is already cashing in with a handsome book deal.

Naturally the people experiencing the brunt of the mental health effects during the pandemic are the same people who experience the brunt of all of our disastrous policies in this country Black and Hispanic people and young people and poorer working people.

The CDC report goes on:

"The percentage of respondents who reported having seriously considered suicide in the 30 days before completing the survey (10.7%) was significantly higher among respondents aged 18–24 years (25.5%), minority racial/ethnic groups (Hispanic respondents [18.6%], non-Hispanic black respondents [15.1%]), self-reported unpaid caregivers for adults (30.7%), and essential workers (21.7%)."

That 10.7% reporting they have seriously considered suicide in just the thirty days before taking the survey is over twice as many as adults (4.3%) who reported considering it in the entire twelve months prior when asked in 2018.

hmm.

I was curious about how people who are sober have been handling the isolation and lack of traditional resources available under the quarantine and the outsized stressors all around us right now but also about how people who are decidedly not sober have gone too far in the other direction which may or may not apply to me personally at this time. I asked a bunch to share their stories of continuing hope or deepening despair and here is a little bit of what they said.

- I work in healthcare and this whole thing has been a shitstorm. I had given up drinking (during the week) for Lent. I'm not very religious, but figured it gives me a reason to give something up for a period. Well anyway, since March 13 when we tested our first positive case, I've been drinking a decent amount each day. It just seems like we are in a nightmare, so why not just drink when I'm not working?
- I'm just waiting for normalcy to return so I can go back to the gym and sleep normal again. That's the part of losing the routine that sucks the most and leads directly to the drinking. If I can go to the gym after work I don't really have the urge to drink. Add no gym and stress at work and it amplifies the urge.
- I just started going to AA meetings in January/February, but once the closings started happening,

the meetings got cancelled. I don't want to look into Zoom online meetings because they're not anonymous (data tracking), and my family would be around hearing them. Thankfully the liquor store is still open. I usually buy a few nips of vodka or tequila. I tell myself it kills the virus, in case I have it. Anyway it's been difficult obviously and my partner is upset about it. Hoping things get better everywhere.

- Eight years of sobriety still intact. The lack of in-person meetings has been rough, but the daily grind has changed so drastically that any theoretical "triggers" pale in comparison.

- My sponsor had actually died somewhere in the midst of it all, and I couldn't attend his funeral because, well, we were reporting on the virus at work. So I emerged from all of this in desperate need to reconnect to the program . . . and my home group had been closed due to the virus. I found one group still open, and it was their last in-person meeting before they shut down. It was very "Rick waking up in The Walking Dead pilot" vibes. Only I'd been awake for it all and didn't know the world had ended just a few miles away. So while everyone else is in a state of stir crazy isolation, I spent the last week with my wife. She drinks, and it doesn't matter. But it's the most I've seen her since we started dating, honestly. Walks in empty parks, gardening, house chores, board games, and reconnecting. Everyone else seems to be going mad and all I've done is heal for the last week. A pandemic is the best thing that ever happened to my emotional sobriety. "Let the tanks roll in," I ended up saying to her. "We've got serenity right here."

- Wednesday this week is four months of sobriety for me. After some rough going early on, I had settled into a pretty good rhythm with it, finding ways to fill my evenings without drinking, thankful for each day without a hangover. Just lately, though, the little bug is back, gnawing at the back of my brain in the late afternoon. Maybe because I fear just how shitty the news is about to get here in North America. I never really got the "drink your sorrows away" thing. Momentarily, maybe, but drinking just helps that shit stack up in my experience. The freedom I found in drinking was purely nihilistic. I just didn't care if I died. Gotta say, that would be a pretty convenient worldview right about now.

- I've been clean (not sober) from heroin for twelve years and this week is a fucking test but also not. I've been thinking about death and all my friends who have died from the opioid epidemic. The apocalyptic mentality of "fuck it I'm gonna have a party" is not a good mindset for an addict. I think these months have been a huge opportunity for relapse for a lot of issues, eating disorders, anxiety, depression, etc. People are alone with their thoughts and demons with few distractions.

- Sobriety is hard enough to maintain under non-pandemic conditions. It's turned up to "Expert Mode" now. Everyone I see on social media is talking about turning to drinking heavily. I hope most of them are joking. I know some aren't. Me, I've been starting to try online meetings. Still going crazy, but a lot less than I would have. One guy was talking about being asked when he was first getting sober what he'd do if it was the post-apocalypse and everyone he loved was gone. He said he thought about it and decided he still wouldn't drink because he didn't want to die an alcoholic death. That helped! Can't control too much right now, but I can fight to avoid that version of the end, anyway.

- I've honestly never felt so connected with my sober community or at least in a long time. Maybe it's because we are all usually so busy with our everyday lives or because we know we're so isolated so we are making more of an effort to stay in touch, but I join Zoom AA meetings every day and also have Zoom "get togethers" with my AA women friends at least every other day. Saturday night we had a "happier hour" and just hung out and chatted for a while on Zoom and we're trying to organize a game night tonight. It makes such a difference staying connected to my AA community this way so that we can talk about what we're feeling and going through during this time without feeling judged or like we're "crazy" or not staying "positive" enough. Only fellow alcoholics understand the way our minds can start to spin and then start rationalizing taking a drink since these are extraordinary times.

· I saw someone post yesterday, "It's not a relapse if it happens under quarantine." I'm almost entirely sure that was a joke, but the thing about alcohol is that it's cunning, baffling, and powerful and can trick us into having thoughts like that and then acting on them. When AA first began, there were only a scattering of meetings across the country so all that most people had was the AA literature and a phone, so I keep reminding myself of that especially when there are people who continuously say that we can't stay sober without in-person meetings and are still meeting up despite all of the warnings and orders that keep getting made. It drives me crazy. Someone said to me the other day that alcohol will kill us before this virus will and that may be true for some but I strongly believe that we are truly fortunate in that we live in an age where we are able to stay connected while staying safe so that neither will kill us.

WE'RE JUST GRATEFUL WE
CAN STILL COME IN AND MAKE
WHAT LITTLE MONEY WE CAN

It's April and although I'm sitting at home many people are not.

"It's forced us all out of our element," a grocery store worker told me. Under normal circumstances he runs the produce department at a popular chain in California. "I'm a workhorse. I order and break heavy pallets of product and organize the shit out of it. That's my thing and I'm good at it."

Now he's something like a combination between a night-club bouncer and a public health official.

"I'm spending hours on end with a clipboard monitoring a line of people in masks that spans a city block, separating them into ten person groups and explaining what they can and can't buy like some post-apocalyptic Disneyland ride operator. Half of my team is allocated to sanitizing carts nonstop and the other half is policing how many eggs and units of raw chicken people have in their carts. It's not traumatic, but talking to your three hundredth masked person in one day takes a toll I didn't anticipate."

"The sudden rise in 'thank yous' we've been getting is nice, but it can't help but feel patronizing, he said. "In the end, we're just grateful we can still come in and make what little money we can."

We talked more about being an essential worker through the first couple months of quarantine.

WALK ME THROUGH A TYPICAL DAY FOR YOU NOW.

My day to day is pretty much completely different than what it used to be. We all get well set into our routines working our normal sections. I've been in charge of produce for over a year. When everything went down, the crazy store rushes, all the madness and shelf-cleaning, corporate took over the ordering, so I was no longer ordering the product myself. That's normally a huge part of the day, getting product in and taking inventory. So it was like what do we do now? We didn't even know what was coming in. That was a pretty big change. Now we're at this level of kind of crowd control. We're not able to get as much stuff as we should, so we have one solid push in the morning to fill what needs we can and with what we have to fill it with. After that it's a lot of standing around. Weirdly it's so much less work physically but more tiring emotionally and mentally.

SO YOU STAND OUTSIDE AND DIRECT PEOPLE TO MAINTAIN A SEPARATION BETWEEN EACH OTHER?

That's a pretty new initiative. We have the line that stretches outside. Our goal is to limit the amount of people we can bring in and enforce social distancing as much as we can. We have six foot markers outside and caution tape on the sidewalk. One of my main duties has been to be outside with a clipboard with all of that day's product restrictions. Every day it changes how many eggs we can allow people to buy versus canned goods. The goal is to stretch things out among the entire community . . . So I group them off into groups of ten and deliver this weird Everybody! Eyes on me! type of speech about how many cases of water I can allow them that day. I explain to them the two people at the front of the line will hand them a freshly sanitized cart or basket. It's been a total role reversal from what we're accustomed to. Guys that would be on register all day are standing by the eggs making sure customers only take one. We can only have every other register open now per social distancing rules.

HOW MANY PEOPLE ARE COMING THROUGH IN A DAY?

We're still getting maybe a thousand. It's hard to say. We're trying to keep maximum capacity of customers in the store at twenty. I let ten people in at a time then we wait til most of them are out. We have so many crew members in there, we can't let too many customers in and compromise the distancing. We let in about seventy people an hour. We're open ten hours a day. Normally it would be thousands of people a day.

YOU SAID SOMETHING LIKE, "WELL, WELL, YEARS OF BEING CRITICIZED FOR NOT USING YOUR DEGREE, AND LOOK WHO'S CONSIDERED ESSENTIAL NOW."

I do have this now sadly justified Good Will Hunting complex about the value of a mechanic over like a day trader. That's always been my kind of blue collar doctrine. I have a degree, 75 percent of my co-workers have degrees, but they fell out of touch with their field or didn't get into that field for whatever reason.

This sense of appreciation all of a sudden is . . . I don't want to say patronizing, but it can feel that way. It's kind of like I've been treated as an underling for so long, so it all feels a little convenient.

DO YOU MEAN PHONEY, LIKE THANKING THE TROOPS?

I don't know, it feels very social media to me. It feels YAS! Twitter-influenced. Which stings.

YOU WERE MORE SCARED OF A SHOOTING THAN THE VIRUS AT FIRST WHEN THIS ALL KICKED OFF?

That crossed my mind. If we were to approach that level of civil unrest . . . I'm 29 and relatively healthy. I don't think about the virus in terms of fear for myself and my well-being, I just gotta go to work. There's nothing I can put between that. I gotta go earn a living. My wife is out of work, she's in the restaurant industry. I do my best, outside of upping my friendliness, washing my hands, and the things we're doing at work, to not think about it all so I can continue doing what I have to do. But I'm more fearful about reaching a level of unrest that would put us in a different kind of physical harm.

WHAT ELSE ARE PEOPLE WORRIED ABOUT?

We all take it differently. We have a lot of people at my store with histories in the healthcare industry that are kind of overall worried about how many people are coming into contact with each other during the day. It's something we're doing everything we can to control but it's still out of control compared to the CDC guidelines. I can tell people all day: "See that yellow x on the ground? I need you to stand on that," but at that point they already have been too close to someone. A manager of mine is trying to limit her hours because she's worried about the store being a hot spot.

ARE YOU STILL BEING COMPENSATED THE SAME?

Compensation is the same, which to me is fine. I saw things about hazard pay, and cool, I'd take more money, but if you told me the Great Depression unemployment rate was 25 percent and we might cross that, but I'm pretty much guaranteed a job, I'd be psyched on that. I'm not going to argue or bite the hand that feeds, which feels weird, the leftist that I am, licking that boot, but I'm appreciative to get work.

ARE YOU GUYS IN A UNION OR TALKING ABOUT ONE?

No, we're not union. I would probably be the one people would approach if there was talk of that. I've been the Bernie surrogate here for the past few months. Our company is very, very good. I hope those reading this understand how rarely I would praise a company. My benefits are insane. It's one of the reasons I continue to work here. We've been clued into a service that can diagnose respiratory symptoms remotely, and we're guaranteed two weeks paid leave, based on symptoms alone, without having to touch our vacation or sick pay. Sure I want more . . . but I understand the reality of things.

THE SHIT TRUMP IS SAYING ABOUT GETTING EVERYONE BACK TO WORK ASAP. WOULD THAT SCARE YOU?

That would be extremely premature in my personal opinion. To think that we're just going to risk millions of lives for the sake of the line on a graph sickens me. It's everything all the Anti-Flag songs I listened to warned me about coming to life.

IS YOUR STAFF YOUNG OR OLD?

We're all the way up man. I work at the store with my father-in-law who is 63. He is holding back right now and not going in, which my management has been cool about. Anyone not comfortable being there is free to stay home without any sort of penalty. Currently they are using their own vacation time to do so. It's still a little gray area, but we are allowed to do what we believe is best for ourselves.

HAVE THERE BEEN ANY FIGHTS OR YELLING IN THE STORE?

Not that I've seen personally. There has been some tension. We had a guy walk around with a baseball bat, so that was like, Ok, I gotta follow that guy around. There's been some tension in lines based on us pulling out seniors and making sure they get sent right in to try to minimize their time in public. For the most part people have been cool. Tensions are high within the crew itself sometimes, but that's just the nature of the times. It's high stress, so it's easy to misdirect frustration. There's been no actual violence, or a time I've had to run toward something or away from something.

WHAT ARE SOME WEIRDLY POPULAR AND UNPOPULAR ITEMS?

We have to keep telling our little jokes between workers while we're there. The running joke is that everything that's still left at the end of the day could probably be discontinued because no one wants it. Sorry I think the shrimp masala bowl might not be the hottest item. The toilet paper thing is still extremely prevalent believe it or not. We get calls all day asking when does it come in. We couldn't get any in March region-wide. Now we can get a couple cases a day. We keep them in the office, allow one per customer, based upon request, and it still sells out within the hour.

I SAW YOU POSTED A REAL SHITTY NOTE FROM YOUR LANDLORD ON TWITTER.

That was one of the most ridiculous things I've read in my entire life. It said rent will be due regardless and they are fully aware the government is supposed to be cutting checks sometime soon. It said we would need proof from our employers that we were financially displaced. My wife would have to get in touch with her managers, aka more red tape for these stressed out people applying for unemployment to jump through, just to prove that this sucks. They said they would set up a payment plan for what we couldn't cover. And it said we do suggest you use these government funds for rent first and foremost, which is horse shit.

NOT GROCERIES.

No, not food or anything you need to live.

I HAVEN'T BEEN TO THE GROCERY STORE IN LIKE TWO WEEKS.

You'll see a big difference. It will be a completely different experience. We are getting a lot of gratitude from customers about the cleanliness of the store, which is nice since we are going above and beyond in that respect. I'm happy to do that. It is just starting to get weird man. You see three hundred masks and you're just like Hey what's up! Have a good one.

It's fucking weird. It's not traumatic. I'm not getting stunned by these freaky thoughts, but I go home and crack open a beer and think, shit that was weird. I see homemade masks, windbreakers wrapped around people's faces. It's just adjusting to how much of it we really see versus a lot of people who have the quarantine privilege which is what I would regrettably call it right now. They're not shielded from it, but speaking to these people in masks every day is kind of harrowing. People who are putting on gloves before they grab the cart. I get it, but it's like, ohh this is all actually happening. We're trying to make the days as normal as possible for us in the store, but sometimes it's just like . . . fuck.

ARE YOU ANGRY WITH THE USELESS PEOPLE LIKE ME WHO GET TO WORK FROM HOME?

I wouldn't call it anger. I would call it a hope that there is some gratitude there as far as the situation goes. I had someone that reached out asking is there anything I can do, and I said "just don't take it for granted." It's not a disdain, it's a call for some perspective. Which I need too. I have a good friend who works at a hospital as a nurse, and her ward just got switched to the Covid ward, which is a different level of perspective for me as well. We just all have this tiered hierarchy for at-risk levels right now, which is strange.

YOU'RE A BIG BERNIE GUY. ISN'T IT INSANE, EVEN SEEING ALL THIS HAPPEN, THAT SO MANY PEOPLE STILL AREN'T LIKE, OH RIGHT, THAT'S THE TYPE OF SHIT WE NEED?

It is beyond maddening. I had a coworker the other day unprompted bring up something I had been espousing normally weeks prior. He was like "I heard you say we're only as healthy as our least insured person." I was like "yes." He said, "what do you mean?" He had no idea there were other countries where every single person has healthcare. That lack of straightforward reporting about healthcare is missing . . . Seeing Biden go missing verses Bernie being out there every day. It's extremely frustrating. Especially after how much all of us put in, to be so swept under the rug is sickening. Especially when we had enacted these policies thirty years ago when he was first fighting for them we would be much better off and prepared right now.

I MISS THOSE PEOPLE VERY MUCH

I remember the first and last time I went to Great Scott it's just the few hundred times in between I'm having trouble keeping track of.

The first time would have been twenty years ago this summer. It was an aggressively average frat bar then not the iconic indie rock club it would soon become and I remember it being terrible and exhilarating but maybe that's just in the way that everything is terrible and exhilarating when you're young. I did not particularly like it at the time it would take a while for that to change.

My friends and I lived across the street in an apartment that smelled like a marmot had pissed all over the rug because that's exactly what had happened with the previous tenants. There would be fights outside on the corner almost every weekend this being the DMZ between Boston College and Boston University and I wasn't particularly interested in finding out what they were about but I'd still go in sometimes anyway because it was right there across the street as I said and the apartment wasn't very comfortable on account of the roaches all over the sink that had migrated over from the Pizzeria Uno next door and the fact that I slept on a random mattress in the living room I had rescued from the sidewalk.

No one really worried about or knew what bed bugs were back then I don't think or maybe I was just twenty one and disgusting.

The last time I ever went was in the winter just before the pandemic for the release party for my first *Hell World* book which was about how capitalism destroys everything and nothing good can stay. The last song I heard there was "Glacier" by my dear friend and sometimes bandmate Aaron Perrino who performed at the release.

It starts so pure
Yeah we dream big
Something happens
Something changes

Like a glacier
That slowly melts away
The hopes we have
Corrode and it starts a tidal wave

"It is with a heavy heart today that I announce that Great Scott will not re-open," long time Great Scott manager Tim Philbin posted on Facebook in May. "For 44 years Great Scott has provided entertainment and more than a few beverages to a loyal group of customers. From its inception in 1976 as a local bar featuring blues and folk performers to the 1980s and 1990s as a beloved college dive featuring cover bands and DJ nights, to the 2000s and its emergence as one of the best live music venues in the city, Great Scott has meant many things to many people."

"Through it all we've aspired to be a good neighbor to our community and a friend to all who walk through our doors. There is a sign that still hangs in the venue from the establishment that Great Scott replaced. The name of which was Brandy's. That sign reads 'Where Incredible Friendships Begin.' I'm glad we never took it down because it explains Great Scott better than I ever could. Take care of yourselves and each other."

It wasn't the first beloved institution in Boston to close because of the economic fall out of the pandemic and it won't be the last but it's the one that has hit me the hardest. Even after we've moved away I always assumed it would be there waiting for me when this is all over.

I've been trying to think about some of the best and worst nights of my life many of which began or ended at Great Scott and I simply can't narrow it down for some reason it's like there's too much static to cut through to find a clean signal. It's like spending a gorgeous day in the ocean many years ago that you generally remember fondly and trying to call to mind right now one specific single wave that buoyed you and a second wave that knocked you over. After a while all the waves become impossible to differentiate from one another and it all flattens out into sensory noise.

The lease for the bar is apparently not going to be renewed by the landlord my other friend and the man mostly responsible for turning Great Scott into what it is Carl Lavin told me. The family who owns the building owns so many other buildings man. When you own that many buildings it's never enough buildings I suppose. Some people spend their lives accumulating real estate and others spend their lives accumulating memories of experiences with friends in shitty bars and then you don't even get to hold onto them for very long on the back end. Unlike real estate memories depreciate in value over time it's a huge fucking rip off.

After a fundraising effort it looks like they may be able to reopen in a different location at some undefined time in the future when we feel safe to congregate again which is hopeful news but it won't really be the same. Nothing will.

It's hard for me to remember anything now due to we've outsourced most of our memories to various devices many of which are no longer even accessible to us. Lost memories on lost memory drives. Most of the memories I have of my life can only be pulled up by a sort of mnemonic tool both in the form of a photo and when the photo is no longer available to me I usually lose the memory too and I guess it just goes on like that until we stop remembering anything at all. Just yesterday we were looking through some old things and we found a black and white photo my grandmother must have taken forty or fifty years ago of the old dilapidated farmhouse I grew up in and she wrote on the back in this shaky little handwriting in faded blue ink "SAVE THIS PHOTO" because I guess even then you needed to document things for them to remain real for as long as possible. I saved the photo though and now I am thinking about her and now she's real again.

I looked at my phone and I saw two toddlers embracing each other in a forest north of Miami and two thirty something women embracing each other in a bathroom mirror on an island west of Oakland and a room full of people singing every word to a song by one of my favorite bands at a show I had tickets to but couldn't bring myself to go to and a Christmas tree and a woman eating dumplings in Chinatown and a friend sharing a photo of himself when he was young and another friend sharing a photo of himself when he was young and then when the news of Great Scott dying from a cocktail of Covid and capitalism came out I saw a video a friend posted from the very show I was talking about not going to which was Piebald. In the video they're singing the song that encapsulates almost everything about this part of my life for me.

"Long nights, hard times, everything that makes you feel tired . . ."

I really wish I had gone to that show now. I fucked up. I fucked up a lot mind you but that is among the more recent ones.

I had to ask some friends to remind me of things I should remember about the club. "First day of spring barbecues on the porch," one said. "Being so coked up and wanting to vomit watching other bands eat McDonald's from across the street," they said.

"[One old friend] getting a beat down outside." "[Another old friend] punching out the dude from [famous band]." "[Another old friend] standing outside smoking with us and then he just . . . died, like eyes rolled up and passed out on the sidewalk. It was weird. A bunch of scumbags trying to figure out what to do, but also being coked up and too nervous to move."

He didn't end up dying to be clear.

"Getting kidnapped by FSU because they thought I was [our other friend]."

Starting to think maybe I did too many drugs and that's why I don't remember anything? Hmm, no it's the other stuff I wrote in here probably. The passage of time shit. Waves and so on like I said. Prettier stuff than brain damage.

I remember loading in to play shows at Great Scott with my various bands over the years and the light shining off the checkerboard floor in the late afternoon sun and the smell which was not as bad as most clubs! Not as bad as marmot piss anyway I can tell you that for sure. I remember the feeling that something could happen not what actually ended up happening specifically but the feeling of anticipating whatever it was it turned out to be.

Then there were of course many times when it just kind of sucked being there being out being anywhere at all it wasn't all hedonism and magical fairy tales about the power of friendship and community or whatever.

Our old bands were all going to take over the world. We didn't of course but we were going to. I remember playing with and watching so many other local bands here who were great and could have done something but didn't for all the reasons that things don't work out the way you planned them.

Actually I take that back about "could have done something" because being part of a local music scene is doing something it doesn't need to lead to anything bigger than that it is in and of itself an accomplishment. Imagine playing a show for anyone anywhere with all your friends there and people actually care at all? What a gift.

We wrote a song back then called "Not Feeling It" for a record called *Life Outside Our Walls* and I've been thinking about it a lot lately under quarantine because it was about being trapped inside a small room afraid to leave and expose yourself to anyone else. If I recall correctly it was actually about cocaine paranoia when I wrote it but that's a pretty safe bet for all the songs we played back then.

That wave metaphor from earlier reminded me I was watching a video this morning called "Carribean Ocean Waves at Night for Sleeping" to try to fall back to sleep with my mind at peace and I read some of the comments like I often do and here's one near the top: "Sitting here drinking wine thinking about everything I should have done. This pandemic makes me think about how we really never have the time we assume we do. Gotta complete goals faster gotta do what you want with your life. Every moment every second."

Michelle and I were trying to list off some of the most memorable shows we saw at Great Scott over the years last night but it's impossible it's like asking someone to name some bands they've heard of. Uh . . . Where do you start? It's like . . . name some books you've read.

You could take a stab at it sure but listing off just a few feels like a failure of sorts like an inability to rise to the occasion because if you narrow it down to this or that it necessarily excludes so much else. I was trying just now to remember some of the fifty or however many it was shows I played myself there in various bands over a decade plus and I can't do it either they're all the same.

I remember the bile in my stomach before a show worrying no one will come and the sort of disappointment I felt when I realized people were actually going to show up because then I had to try hard.

When I close my eyes and picture Great Scott I keep waking up in the bathroom. It was a shitty bathroom to do drugs in to be honest the stall barely locked and the line was always pretty long particularly on Friday nights for The Pill the long running and greatest dance party in Boston in my lifetime and the night where I made most of my best friends in the Boston music world many of which I am still close to to this day. I don't particularly miss those friends right now during quarantine because I can talk to them and text them or dial them up on the video conference but all the other people the people I barely cared about or did care about but not quite enough to make it an official friendship? I miss those people very much.

Alvvays. An early show by them is jumping out at me as I think about this. Glasvegas too for some reason. I wonder why I remember those ones more than the others. Probably because I still have pictures of them. Passion Pit. Piebald. MGMT. Nothing. Pup. Pianos Become the Teeth. Speedy Ortiz.

I asked my friend Tom just now to remind me something about those early days in that shitty apartment across from Great Scott.

"My favorite story about that place besides the marmot piss was when they were trying to show the apartment before we moved out, and I was unemployed, you worked nights and Raj was on summer break from school and they came by at like 11 a.m. and we were all just lounging around in our own filth and their contempt for us was so palpable."

Also he said "you burned a hole in the rug one time because you were lighting money on fire." I don't remember that at all. I don't remember having any money to spend never mind light on fire but it was the 2000s I don't know what to tell you.

Sometime a few years after I moved out of the roach apartment and was living in the maggot apartment down the street with like seven other people and showering in a backed-up tub full of brown water Carl Lavin told me he wanted to turn Great Scott into a rock club and I said good luck with that idiot or something like that probably nicer than that. I didn't think it was going to work and I wonder if he ever remembered that the following three hundred or so times I stood next to him over there at the far end of the bar where he kept his laptop and checked his fantasy baseball scores or whatever it was he was doing. I'd peak around the corner to catch a minute of whoever it was who was playing. These guys are actually good I'd say to him when it was true which was more often than you might expect for a little rock club like that. These guys are actually pretty good.

I imagine they'll be putting in another bank branch or some dog shit in the Great Scott space soon because once this is over the pre-pandemic gentrifying and homogenizing forces already long conspiring to destroy anything with character in Boston and Allston in particular will have had their way. It will be right across the street from the other

fancy bank branch that's already there right now and someday no one will tell any stories whatsoever about going there
for their banking needs. They won't even have any memories
to forget like I did.

I SWAM MY STUPID LITTLE LAPS AT THE POOL I'LL NEVER SWIM IN AGAIN

If you take a left out of my new house onto the street that looks like they airdropped a cramped Cape Cod neighborhood into the middle of Central Massachusetts then crossed the road where the cars fly by so fast due to a pandemic means traffic accidents can't happen anymore I guess and head down toward the old wool mill that looms over the town no pun intended and run by the rushing Assabet which I think means "the place where the river turns back" in Algonquian where the swarming little black bugs plague me and get stuck in my beard and keep going toward the town center where the lonely delivery drivers in masks lurk in the quiet doorways of the handful of struggling restaurants still open the Indian one smells so good from like three blocks away and end up on the bike trail that stretches for about ten miles through five different old mill towns around here and which I gather commuters used to bike on to get to the train to Boston back when people still commuted you'll come to a house I pass by every day on my run with a giant TRUMP MAGA FUCK YOUR FEELINGS flag in that disgusting color blue like if you mixed tequila with Gatorade and puked it out hung for everyone who passes by to see and every time you encounter it you'll think anew all over again ah what the fuck and you will feel unwelcome in the place you live now which is the point of any such Trump sign it's to make certain people feel unwelcome and uneasy it's like if you stumbled upon the headless corpse of a brigand hung outside the castle walls you'd think we gotta get out of here man this place seems like bad news they don't treat people right here.

"I'm not one for saying a city is 'dead,' I mean most of our cities existed during the 1918 flu and rebounded," a friend just tweeted. "But Boston, like most cities, is going to be totally different when we re-emerge, and for the first time in 22 years, I'm considering if I want to emerge somewhere else."

It's September and the list of beloved longstanding bars and restaurants closing down for good in Boston and Cambridge keeps growing.

But by the time I'd arrived twenty years ago I thought it was already over. That was the sense I had anyway. That the Boston I now inhabited was some imperfect and diminished version of what had come before. Shuttered clubs and bars and diners where matters of significant local folklore had transpired and defined life for the previous generation were lost to time they said.

This likely happened in whatever city you came of age in as well it's the same story anywhere. Everything was always some degree better before in a time you no longer have access to. This is a lie in many ways and a story people tell themselves to mythologize their own youth but it can also be true. Things can and do very often get worse.

They can also get better though and so you nonetheless find your own places and make of them what you can and conspire in the erection of new monuments to joy and then twenty years on as the marriage of progress and entropy has its sour way with your life this time you pass on this sense of disappointment to your younger friends who listen but only so much. You know things but you don't know everything. You know what happened but you don't necessarily know what is happening.

A neighborhood's soul is lost then rebuilt then lost again and it goes on and on but there is I think a potential end point where the predictions of a neighborhood's demise can finally be fulfilled and maybe that's here for Boston and for similar cities. Places with an abundance of soul can drag out the process for a long time but there are only so many blows they can take. My beloved Harvard Square has continued to be a cultural destination for all these years of loss simply because there was so much to lose in the first place. Now every other storefront is a bank branch.

When a room slowly starts to fill with water you can continue to float upward and breathe until the very end when you're left scraping at the last pocket of oxygen. Things used to be better in this sunken room you think and then you go under.

It's April and it's raining like it's a funeral for a superhero and Michelle is hiding in the car in the driveway of our new place because she's afraid to go near the movers only one of whom is wearing a mask. I'm not supposed to be helping them lift heavy things because of my back and also the virus of course but masculinity is a powerful drug man and so I do and of course I hurt myself in the process. On the load out of the old place we opened up the big front windows that always let in a biting draft in the winter and hurled everything we weren't holding onto into the yard and it smashed and splintered and piled into a temporary junkyard of our years of accumulated memories.

I own a tree now. One single tree in a tiny backyard. I'm not thinking about the house in terms of it being mine because I don't really own it I am simply borrowing it from a bank and in any case it does not feel like my home it's some empty rooms to put my shit in. The tree is mine to do with as I please however and it's majestic. It's a royal maple Michelle just told me when I asked. The home is a village colonial she told me. I am not the kind of person who knows the names of trees or styles of homes. I guess they built the street we live on about 150 years ago as housing for workers at the mill which sits mostly empty and quiet now. This entire town is quiet although I'm honestly not sure if that's its natural state or if it's because of the pandemic. I have no before frame of reference to judge things by everything is just like this now.

The delivery options are absolute fucking shit out here too.

It's August and newspapers are writing stories about "everyone fleeing the cities" and by everyone they mean rich people who never belonged to the city in the first place they were just briefly consumers there. Our move had nothing to do with the virus to be clear it was already planned but it feels momentous all the same. I was so so angry when I found out the bid we put on this home was accepted. Michelle and I had one of our worst fights in a long time over it. I never thought it was going to be real. I thought I'd be going to my favorite places that don't exist anymore for years to come. Now I feel like I've abandoned my people and my places but maybe moving to a much less densely packed suburb just as a pandemic exploded in cities in the northeast was an accidental stroke of genius. I was supposed to be sitting here in the desolate wasteland complaining that there is nothing to do and nowhere to go but now everywhere is desolate and there is nothing to do and nowhere to go anywhere.

I read that there were four cases in our new town the other day. Some high school kids had gone to a graduation party they weren't supposed to.

After living in our old apartment for thirteen years owing mostly to the fact that the nice old lady downstairs liked us and rarely raised the rent as much as others would have we were finally forced out once her daughter took over and wanted to gut the place and double the rent and so we were looking for a long time for a home to borrow because if we're going to have to pay like $2,500 a month or more to rent now we might as well pay it as a mortgage instead and so finally we found one about forty minutes west of Boston in a nice little town with at least three Dunkin' Donuts that I am aware of and probably more.

Looking for a house is very strange it's like a form of temporary time travel. Every home you do not buy or every apartment you do not move into is a closing off of a potential future you imagined for yourself however briefly. The light in here is very nice you think as you're walking from room to room. I could see myself living in that light for a long time you think. And then you find out someone else came in and offered like $50,000 more in cash than they were asking and you go ah well I guess I'll just go fuck myself and keep looking for slightly worse places to live in towns you've never heard of. Then you convince yourself the place you wanted sucked anyway to soothe the loss of that potential life you had briefly imagined for yourself within those walls. Fuck that place you think. Fuck that potential life we might have made there. It's like when you get rejected or dumped by someone and instantly all of their flaws you had managed to overlook become readily apparent.

Sometimes you look at a house or apartment or condo and the fucking guy in the suit is showing you how the light switch works and you're going haha and he's going haha and you go how recently was the vinyl siding put on and he says I'll have to check and then you walk around and you see a room and your entire life expands to fill that room. 250 square feet of a life and you think I could see myself dying in this room someday but you won't you're going to die in some other room and you don't know what it looks like yet. Some room you can afford to die in.

I'm sad that I never got a last chance to do any of the things I regularly did in my old neighborhood because of the lockdown like I'll never see my barber again I'll never go to our beloved local pub again and I'll never take the bus into Harvard Square on an early spring day when everyone is outside to sit there and just watch people moving around like they used to do in the before times.

I didn't even get to do any of the stuff I've done all the time for over a decade one last time while knowing it was the last time if that makes sense but I suppose that is how things go you never know when it's the official last time for anything. I could drive back and take one last see you later lap to all my places but it won't be the same because they aren't mine anymore.

One of the things we had talked about months ago was how it was going to be sad to say goodbye to the old lady downstairs when the time came but then we didn't even get to do that because she's like ninety and it's didn't seem like a good idea to come into contact with her in case we were infected so instead we just knocked on the window to the room where she sits downstairs with the TV blasting and waved and said byeeeee thank you so much for being (relatively) good to us all these years and she said what? because she can't hear anything and we waved again and maybe she registered that we were gone or maybe she didn't and now we're somewhere else and soon enough we'll all be somewhere else.

We have a new old neighbor now. Every morning I go out on the porch to smoke and he's there fiddling around with this or that and I say hello and he says hello and he says can you believe all this and I tell him I cannot.

IT TRULY IS INNOCENCE

I don't care about children. Wait that doesn't sound right. I don't have any children and so because of that I spend almost no time thinking about them. But for whatever reason a question has been lingering with me lately which is: How do you explain to kids why all of a sudden everything is different for them? Do kids understand what a pandemic is?

I asked a bunch of parents what it is they said to their kids specifically. I was curious mostly what language they used.

- The hardest has been walking by playgrounds and telling her that we can't swing or slide because they're "broken."

- Our kid is five years old, in pre-school. I'd say he's a bit more cognizant of the world around him than most, maybe because we don't sugarcoat most things, or baby him. We basically told him that it affects mostly older people, so he wouldn't worry too much. We explained how viruses work etc., pretty scientific type conversations about it. My wife is a pharmacist so we have been pretty worried she'd bring it home. We had been listening to a lot of news/podcasts in the beginning but all the talking about death and dying was too much for him, so he started saying "The news is horrible! I hate the news!" One day we were sitting on the couch and he said "You know, the coronavirus isn't so bad. Now I don't have to go to all those terrible places with you." I'm always dragging him to Wegmans and Home Depot and shit because my wife works thirteen hours a day. Other days when he really wants to go to Chuck E. Cheese, he raises a fist and shouts "Curse you, coronavirus!" up at the sky.

• I don't have a separate strategy for talking about the virus with my ten-year-old daughter. I've always had a general policy that, whenever she asks me about something, however weird or horrible, I'll tell her. And if there's a situation where me withholding context would be the same as lying, I'll fill her in then, too (like explaining what a nuke is, etc.). So I've tried to warn her that people are still getting sick and that school might not be back to normal for another year. But kids are very elastic and adaptive. She mostly just doesn't seem to care.

• We have six and four year olds. We pretty much lay out the facts, talk about the virus, and how this one is new. We say that they are not in danger from this virus, but there are people in our community who could get very sick and that we are trying to protect them with various social distancing protocols. They do ok with this. But my four year old heartbreakingly told me that she misses hugging, and when the "sickness" is gone the first thing she'll do is give everyone hugs. Oof.

- I told my four year old there is a sickness going around and we do not want to get the germs. Did a lot of extra attention on handwashing and "germ awareness." She refers to it as "the sickness" and is scared and sad sometimes. It's a lot to handle when you have limited life experience.

- We say "the big sick" with our almost three year old. She doesn't really get it but she relearned habits quickly. She no longer asks to go to playgrounds or stores, etc. At first she would say "I want to go somewhere!" And at first they tried to do Zoom meetings for the preschool friends, and she quit. She said "I want to see the real friends."

- I have a nine-year-old daughter and a four-year-old son. Kind of unsurprisingly to me, the kids have adjusted . . . really well? I mean they watch too much TV now but I guess fuck it because everything is going to shit. When everything is Normal, I'm a barista, but I've been out of work for a couple of months. I've been living off of my tax return and we're doing ok, much better than a lot of people. It's wild because my kids and I actually have time to play. I'm not exhausted from standing for eight hours a day, and I actually have the energy to act like an evil alien queen from outer space or whatever they've decided they want me to be when they tackle me to the ground in the backyard. They beg to go to the beach because to them this is an early summer, but they take it relatively well when I explain why we can't go. I'm kind of dreading going back to work. I know I can't stay home forever because we can't eat if I don't make money, but I'm going to miss having this time with my kids. I don't know how well any of us will adjust to that.

- I told my kids there's a very bad disease going around, it doesn't hurt kids, but it's dangerous for old people and sick people. We all have to stay inside to make sure the people who are weaker than we are don't get sick. The kids now want to know why their friends are allowed to play together and they aren't. It's a mess. I'm trying not to say those people are just assholes, but the seven year old gets it. He says they must not really care what happens to other people.

- I don't know how to explain to my two-and-a-half year so he can understand. I don't want to scare the shit out of him by trying. We've been calling masks "superhero masks," that's all we got so far.

- My oldest son will be five this summer. My wife and I have been using the term "germ bugs" to explain why we stay inside, but we had to tweak the concept so that he felt like he could go out into our fenced-in backyard. That was after he yanked my one-and-a-half year old away from the open side door to "protect him from the germ bugs." In simple terms, we basically explain that we are trying to keep other people from getting sick, because I don't want him worrying about getting sick himself. We haven't mentioned anything about death, but at the same time during this quarantine our cat died. So we had to explain that. It's been pretty fucked up over here. The oldest is six, the young one is only two. At first it was difficult when we walked by parks and playgrounds but when I explained that he was helping people by not playing on them he's been awesome. Kids are really honest and surprisingly want to help. Adults are a different story. Also, this has made him grow an appreciation for listening to the Ramones by ourselves in the driveway. Talking about death is the toughest though, because of the finality of it. He wants to make sure no people die because of him and wonders why others haven't done the same. It truly is innocence.

I HUGGED HER AND PRETENDED THAT COULD NEVER HAPPEN TO US

I'm having such vivid dreams lately probably because it's my only opportunity to go anywhere.

I wished on a monkey's paw a few months back that looking at Twitter for nineteen hours a day and getting drunk every night would become more socially acceptable. I should not have done that and I'm sorry.

I'm going to get the stupidest tattoo when this is over. Yes even stupider than the ones I already have.

When I woke up this morning Michelle was crying because she said one of her colleagues' husband died and she couldn't even go to see him in the hospital and then I hugged her and pretended that could never happen to us but I was lying.

I was on the new porch last night and a couple appeared out of nowhere in the middle of the street just over there to my left and I think we startled each other and then they said oh hello and I said oh hello and they were standing there staring up at the sky and I guess there was a noteworthy moon of some kind transpiring that they were very invested in. I went to look myself after they had gone because it felt weird to go stand and stare at the sky just because some other people were doing it and also there is the distancing matter to consider and then there it was some kind of moon with a name I've never heard of. A big moon in any case. I've had enough of new types of moons if I'm being honest like when you stop becoming interested in new music at a certain point in your life that's how I feel about moons. I know all the moons I'll need to know at this juncture I think. So I stood there and thought about Donald Barthelme and said to myself See the moon? It hates us.

Yesterday we went for our first walk in the area in what we thought was going to be a lovely nature reserve due to when you look at it on the Google Map it's this giant green space and when we got there there were lots of trails and paths and things but it looked more like a place teenagers would go to drink exactly one beer and finger each other for a minute then get nervous a guy with an axe was hiding behind a rock. Are kids still afraid of men with axes coming around in the woods like we used to be or is it just the guns now? You used to have to be murdered in the woods when I was young now I guess it can happen anywhere. The land we were on was of course home to Native Americans originally then taken by colonists in the 1600s and then Thoreau fucked around nearby some time later.

I guess a bunch of Revolutionary War shit happened around here who can keep it all straight. When you live in Massachusetts every other fucking thing has some grave importance to the founding of the country. Then during World War II the government took the land by eminent domain because they thought it was in the national interest to do so and they built a bunch of ammunition bunkers that were close enough to the train lines to get to Boston but far enough away from the water that German battleships wouldn't be able to reach them. They call the bunkers igloos and I saw one yesterday as I was jogging by and people had spray-painted Fuck Trump on it and penises and so on all the usual stuff people spray-paint on things and it just occurred to me now I have never lived this far away from the ocean and maybe that is what is wrong with me lately. Typically every night I wake up about two or three times and have to put a relaxing TV show on the laptop so my brain doesn't have one second to go where it wants to go if I don't stop it but last night I remembered you can listen to soothing white noise things so I found this <u>video</u> of the waves and the wind on some beach in the French Mediterranean and it actually worked the fucking video of the waves and the wind tricked my worm brain into thinking I was somewhere safe and calm and not on a mattress on the floor in a strange bedroom that's mine but isn't really quite yet.

"If things get crazy, I will just live in a tent on a beach in Galveston and fish and surf the rest of my life," someone commented on the video of the waves and the wind about a month ago just as things indeed did get crazy. "Be careful out there," someone replied. "Things have changed at the Beach. I lived in Galveston most of my life. Used to love fishing. It's amazing what comes crawling out at night behind the big boulders."

"Am I the only one terrified of this deep watery abyss creeping in on us?" someone else wrote.

The wildlife refuge we went to yesterday was designated an EPA Superfund cleanup site in the 1990s due to there was arsenic and pesticides and other shit all over the place but now I'm sure it's all fine! There was a young family there in the parking lot when we were leaving the girls were probably like seven or six or something and were all excited to have a picnic and they jumped into the back hatch of the SUV and the mother said hold on let me set it up nice and she laid out a blanket on the tailgate so it would seem like a realer type of picnic to them and it broke my heart a little bit and it made me think a lot of parenting is pretending things are nice for the kids who are generally too stupid to know any better.

Oh wait I forgot the reason why I brought up the couple in the street last night that startled me with their moon-looking was that since we haven't really been able to properly meet any of our new neighbors everyone is suspicious to me and whenever one of them lumbers into my perspective or trots by with a silly unworried dog it's unsettling. In a city you see strangers all the time and it's normal they become invisible you bump into them on the street and on the subway without even noticing what they look like we all smash around like blind bats using our other senses to echolocate trouble but in the suburbs any new person you see you think ok who's this fucking guy. Maybe I'm just on edge because I went to sign into the Wi-Fi the other day and I saw one of the nearby networks was named TRUMP2020 and another was TRUMPKAG and now on top of worrying about which of the people around me might be carrying the invisible coronavirus I have to wonder which one is carrying that particular virus too.

Here's a post I just saw on Facebook from a doctor in New York.

"'Who's going to pay for it?'"

"Last words I'll never forget // the response my patient gasped out (between labored breaths) to me and my team, after we explained that he needed to be intubated and placed on a ventilator. We then called his wife to have him speak to her for what was likely his last opportunity, as many patients do not recover once tubed."

"This situation is by far the worst thing I've witnessed in my collective 12 years of critical care & anesthesia. Next-level heartbreak = having to hear a dying patient use his last words to worry about healthcare finances."

"This country is truly a failed state, and it's so sickening to witness firsthand, more blatantly than ever."

At least seventy patients at a veterans care facility in Massachusetts died within the span of a few weeks this spring. A dozen or so other veterans and staffers there also tested positive.

The first death reportedly came at the beginning of the pandemic but it seems that some combination of incompetence or indifference and callousness led management at the facility to downplay the spread and hide it from local officials. It wasn't until an anonymous tip came in to the city's mayor that news of the conditions became widely known.

"No one at City Hall had been told of the deaths before last weekend," Holyoke mayor Alex Morse told the *Boston Globe*.

It's August now and Morse who is running for Congress against one of our absolute worst Richard Neal is being rat-fucked with a phony sex scandal smear. It's September now and he lost.

Around that time I spoke with the grandson of an elderly Alzheimer's patient living at the facility. They didn't learn that he had tested positive or that there was even any reason to test him until just before the story broke in the media. Even then they weren't told about the increasing number of deaths he said.

"There was never any discussion about deteriorating circumstances around there or more cases," he told me. "They said they were aware there was one case, and that was all that had been disclosed to my mother."

Employees had reportedly been complaining for weeks that the facility did not seem to be taking the virus seriously. One said they were disciplined for wearing a mask while treating a patient who had been confirmed positive according to the *Globe*.

"Your actions are disruptive, extremely inappropriate and have caused unnecessary resources to be deployed that may be needed in the future," the disciplinary letter read. "Your behavior unnecessarily disrupted and alarmed staff."

I wonder what the last normal thing any of those folks in the home did before they realized they were being sent there? I wonder if they knew before it was too late?

I asked people in April what the last normal mundane thing they remember doing was before they fully realized what was up with the pandemic. Here's some of what they said.

- Taking the last two jars of whole peeled tomatoes at the grocery store, feeling guilty and putting one back for someone else.

- Took the kids ice skating the first weekend of March. Felt uneasy seeing people cough. That was kinda the moment.

- I worked a shift behind the bar and remember the false confidence of everyone drinking and dismissing this like just another headline that wouldn't affect them.

- I was one of those people on the other side of the bar on a Friday, before Ohio shut the bars down on a Sunday afternoon. It wasn't a disrespect for what was going on, it's just what I always did. Then the gravity of everything fell on me that weekend.

- I ate lunch in a room with 150 people on a film set. Passed gear around like we normally would with multiple people touching it. Put my slate marker in my mouth while filling out a camera report. It all seems unfathomable now.

- I interviewed at a bar on March 13th and elbow bumped the manager to accept the job. I worked the next day and by Wednesday it was closed indefinitely.

- My birthday party at an escape room. We escaped the room now there is no escape.

- Went for Szechuan food in a deserted restaurant in Sunset Park with my best friends. Tried to get my boyfriend to come with us, arguing it was going to be the last normal day . . . and it was.
- I was on vacation at the beginning of the month and it's really like I flew back home into the alternate universe.
- I met friends for dinner and then watched *Uncut Gems* at their house and ever since then it's frankly like the *Uncut Gems* stress never left me.
- Going to the playground, pushing my kid in one of those grimy plastic seats that's nasty under the best of circumstances. No more of that!
- Saw toilet paper on store shelves and thought, "Eh, I'll grab some tomorrow." Swiftly regretted that.
- Going to Cheesecake Factory. I wish I had a better memory.
- Visited my mom. She's alone and lonely. I can't risk seeing her now and feel so bad.
- Giving my friend a hug.

EVEN THOUGH WE DIDN'T LIVE
NEAR THE OCEAN ANYMORE

It's April and I swaddled my head in cloth like a fragile vase I wanted to ship across the country and walked to the 7-Eleven for the first time in a long time and it was invigorating to Go Out it felt like a trip to fucking Paris.

I still haven't been watching much cable news lately. I can barely bring myself to look at CNN or MSNBC so I'm certainly not going to be keeping up with Fox News on a regular basis. I haven't been watching much of anything to be honest basically I wake up every morning and say ah fuck motherfucker then I drink coffee and smoke cigarettes and listen to Duke Ellington or some shit like that to relax until it's late enough in the day that I can reasonably drink Johnny Walker Black and smoke cigarettes and listen to 2000s nu-metal to gas myself up.

Typically in between I'll go for a run then come home and do some shitty little push-ups and think alright now I've earned this feast of shitty cheddar cheese and Triscuits. Then around 8 p.m. I'll take exactly one hit of my weed pen and pass out and start the whole thing over again. The perfect system.

The most normal shit has taken on a foreboding air. Birds are out here fucking and sucking each other off all over the trees because it's springtime and not for any other apocalyptic reason and yet it's frightening now to hear them scream at each other in their idiot sky language. Maybe it's scary in part because they seem capable of carrying on very well without us either way.

It's May and Michelle is downstairs conducting her class over the computer which she has done the past few mornings while I lay in bed trying to think of a reason to get out of it and coming up short. Yesterday the class was on how to have proper etiquette online how to not be a troll and so forth and I thought haha I should probably take that class too. Or maybe she could have me come by in like a scared straight capacity like when they used to bring a recovered addict to talk to your school about drugs and you wouldn't take it seriously because when you're a kid addiction is like a mortgage or something it's something that happens to adults someday far off down the line that doesn't matter to you now. It's like when you're reading the instructions on the Google Map thing when you're driving on a long trip and the third or fourth item down is a weird turn you'll need to pay attention to at some point but not just yet it's still forty miles away. In any case I have both those things now all the addictions you could handle and the mortgage and I'd just as soon I didn't but too late now on both accounts.

Here's what I want I want to walk into a bar and sit down next to some fucking guy and be annoyed by every single little movement he makes and every comment about what's playing on the TV. I want me to want him to shut the fuck up. I want to have the bartender ask me how I am and

I want to tell them not too bad man and mean it. I want to wheel a carriage with a fucked up wheel down the aisle of the grocery store and find someone standing in front of the vast array of Cheez-It options taking their sweet ass time deciding and I want to think hurry up with the Cheez-Its Jesus Christ. I want to peel off my clothes in a room full of gross old man dicks and balls and climb into my shorts and walk to the pool and hurl myself into it and swim back and forth going nowhere just moving through the water. I want to be dragged to a dinner party I would prefer not to go to and sit there on someone's stupid couch and reach a pita chip over and scrape it across the bowl of hummus and say ha ha that's wild when someone is telling me a story about whatever cute little job they have and I want to go meet a friend I haven't seen in a while and sort of not feel like it all day but then realize halfway through the visit that I love them and there's a reason why I still know them even after all these years. Then once I've done all that once I've talked and talked I want to go home and be alone for a little while like it's a pleasure I've earned not a punishment we're all suffering through.

Then maybe a year or two from now I want to come down with a fever and think ah fuck I've got a very normal and regular fever and crawl into bed for a day or two and guzzle some Nyquil and watch stupid movies on my laptop and not think it's the end of anything rather just how things go sometimes and then many years after that perhaps thirty-five to forty of them if I'm lucky I want to come down with a worse fever or something and think ah fuck and crawl into a hospital bed and die with my wife being allowed to stand by my side thinking about how nice all those years were even though we didn't live near the ocean anymore.

DURING A PANDEMIC PEOPLE ARE GOING TO BE LOOKING FOR ANY SORT OF HOPE

I talked to a guy who watches hours of Fox News every day like it's his job because it actually is. His name is Bobby Lewis and he works for Media Matters. Honestly that job seems like sort of a nightmare to me but I was curious about how they've been covering the pandemic and what sorts of fucked up dog shit they are poisoning people's brains with of late regarding the virus.

SERIOUSLY THOUGH HOW DOES IT MAKE YOU FEEL?
It's tiresome for sure. It's exhausting to watch these people do what they do. We try to find ways to push back where we can. Without trying to blow too much smoke up my own ass, it feels important in times like these. Medical misinformation is always bad, especially during a pandemic, and we'll call it out when we see it.

YOU GUYS PUT OUT A BIG TIMELINE OF ALL THE MISINFORMATION ON SOME OF THE CURES THEY'VE BEEN TALKING ABOUT?
Fox has been talking an awful lot about chloroquine and hydroxychloroquine, two different medications that have had various uses for a while now. But they've latched onto

them as potential treatments for COVID-19. There is mixed and anecdotal spotty evidence that they may have a positive effect. It seems like something generally worth looking into, but Fox being Fox, the tone of the coverage is more like snake oil salesmen pushing miracle cures. One of the first times that it came out was Laura Ingraham talking about it having a Lazarus effect on people.

A BIT OVERSTATED.

A bit overstated. During a pandemic people are going to be looking for any sort of hope that they can find, because this sucks for everybody. But you just can't go around saying those things, giving people hope, when the evidence is not quite there yet.

I'VE WRITTEN BEFORE ABOUT HOW SOME OF MY FAMILY WATCH FOX NEWS, OR AT LEAST GET NEWS FROM SOME SKETCHY RIGHT-WING FACEBOOK SOURCES. BUT THEY'RE TAKING THIS SERIOUSLY, THEY'RE NOT IDIOTS, THEY ARE STAYING HOME AND DOING ALL THE RIGHT THINGS. BUT EVERY NOW AND AGAIN SOMETHING WILL COME THROUGH WHERE THEY'LL SAY, LIKE, "BUT MAYBE THE MEDIA IS PLAYING THIS UP?" ETC. YOU CAN ALMOST SEE TWO PARTS OF A PERSON'S BRAIN IN CONFLICT WITH ONE ANOTHER WHEN THAT HAPPENS. THERE'S THE RATIONAL MIND, THE SCIENCE-BELIEVING SIDE, AND THEN ANOTHER PART WHICH MUST BE COMING FROM PEOPLE ON FOX NEWS AND PEOPLE LIKE THEM DOWNPLAYING THINGS.

Yeah, if there are two top lines to Fox's coverage, alongside the hydroxychloroquine campaign has been the idea that Trump is and always has been doing a great job. Everybody saying otherwise is just out to get him. They don't want to give him a win. It's applying that same old perpetual victim framework to the pandemic. I think that might be the conflict that you're seeing.

[BY THE WAY IT'S LATE JULY NOW AND AFTER A FEW MONTHS OF LAYING OFF THE HYDROXYCHLOROQUINE STUFF TRUMP HAS TROTTED OUT SOME GROUP OF CURSED DOCTOR GHOULS ONE OF WHOM BELIEVES PEOPLE ARE POISONED BY DEMON SEMEN OR SOMETHING TO START HYPING IT ANEW . . . OK NOW IT'S APRIL AGAIN.] HOW HAS THE GENERAL ARC OF THEIR COVERAGE GONE? IT STARTED OUT AS "THIS IS ALL NOTHING." HAS IT PROGRESSED?

Sort of. They started off downplaying it and saying this coronavirus is a hoax to take down Trump . . . After that it seemed to start to go into, "Sure, this might not be good, but worst case it could be the flu." Once they finally had to start taking it seriously, Fox & Friends at least did start having more doctors on the air, and doing more human interest stories. Stepping up to support our healthcare workers . . . or our local restaurants that are struggling. But they're still doing the hydroxychloroquine campaign, and now with some of these anti-social distancing protests some of the hosts are latching onto that. One of them, an analyst, Andrew Napolitano, was on Fox & Friends playing up the Michigan stay at home order like it was a life or death moment for American liberty. He said something like If we don't take our freedoms back now we might not ever get them back!

This is not a permanent situation anyone! Nobody's freedoms are permanently threatened by a stay at home order. Everyone wants it to be temporary. I just don't understand what the big freak out is.

IF YOU WERE TO BE FAIR, WHAT IS THE COMPLETELY NON-IDIOTIC ARGUMENT THAT THEY'RE ACTUALLY MAKING? I SEE A LOT OF PEOPLE SAYING SHIT LIKE "THIS IS WHAT SOCIALISM IS!?" WHAT DO THEY ACTUALLY THINK THE PLOT IS HERE? TO MAKE EVERYONE DESTITUTE SO WE HAVE TO LOOK FOR THE GOVERNMENT FOR HELP?

It never seems to make much sense when they try to tie all the threads together. I have heard the entire coronavirus is being cheered on by the media because it's going to make Trump look bad. But if people turn to the government for help that's an opportunity for Trump to help and look good! There's just so many conspiratorial strands embraced by folks who don't seem to be able to get out of that mode of thinking.

SOMEONE ACTUALLY GOT FIRED . . . WHAT WAS THAT, SHE WASN'T THAT POPULAR, AND THEY WERE JUST THROWING SOMEONE TO THE WOLVES.

Trish Regan. I think that's what that was. I haven't seen much reporting about what happened inside Fox News. She ran that ridiculous coronavirus impeachment scam segment at the top of March. Her show was pulled off the air, ostensibly, to make more room for straight news coronavirus coverage. Fox was very insistent her show had not been canceled. Then like a week later she was fired. It seems like she sailed a little too close to the sun. Something like that Sean Hannity absolutely could've gotten away with. But Trish Regan on Fox Business just doesn't have the clout Hannity has. She was expendable, he isn't.

YOU PRIMARILY WATCH IN THE MORNING. BUT AS FAR AS YOU CAN TELL WHICH OF THE PERSONALITIES ARE DOING THE WORST JOB IN TERMS OF THE VIRUS INFORMATION?

I'd say it's a pretty neck and neck race between Hannity and Ingraham. Hannity was a big early downplayer. Now he's on this little crusade saying he's always taken it seriously, just like President Trump, and it's actually the media that's been downplaying it the whole time. Meanwhile Laura Ingraham is out here making it like she was the biggest early pusher of hydroxychloroquine, and her fucking sidekick, Raymond Arroyo, on Fox Nation, said this ridiculous shit: He suggested that hospitals are inflating the death tolls from COVID-19, because they get more money if people die from it. It's just fucking bananas.

IT'S JUST LIKE . . . WHAT MONEY!?

Right? From where. Who is giving the hospitals the Covid death checks? Where is it coming from?

I FIND MYSELF DESPAIRING A LITTLE BIT THINKING ABOUT THIS. EVEN THOUGH WE ALL KNOW HOW TERRIBLE FOX NEWS IS, YESTERDAY I WAS THINKING, LIKE, WE CAN'T EVEN DECIDE ON A SET OF FACTS DURING THIS POTENTIALLY WORLD-ALTERING PANDEMIC? EVEN THOUGH IT'S SOMETHING I KNEW BEFORE . . . IF ALIENS ARRIVED OR SOMETHING. WOULD WE EVEN BE ABLE TO HAVE THE SAME FRAME OF REFERENCE ON THAT?

Absolutely. I think about that a lot too. I still don't have any answers.

WHAT'S SOME OF THE OTHER DUMBEST SHIT YOU'VE HEARD?

A month ago or so Jerry Falwell Jr. was on talking about maybe North Korea got together with the Chinese to release this coronavirus in America. I think that was the same show where the host Ainsley Earhardt opened the show saying the pandemic was actually the safest time to fly because all the airports were so empty and that everyone should go get a plane ticket. It's just so . . . breathtaking. I don't know how to explain to someone that when a disease is ravaging the planet it's not a good time to get on an airplane. You either understand it or you don't. I don't know how to explain it.

ISN'T THERE A CONFLICT BETWEEN WHAT FOX IS SAYING INTERNALLY TO EMPLOYEES ABOUT HOW SERIOUSLY TO TAKE THIS AND THE MESSAGE THEY'RE PUTTING OUT TO PEOPLE?

Oh yeah. I'm not sure if there's textual differences, but absolutely in the general tone of the coverage. Internally Fox News seems to be like "This is very serious, it's probably going to be going on for a long time, and we're not sure when we'll be able to get back to normal." Whereas Fox News broadcasting is like "This is a very serious time, but it's been going on for so long, we need to end it as soon as we can." It seems like they agree on the premise, but the conclusions are wavering so differently.

THERE'S THIS WEIRD CONFLICT I HAVE. SOMETIMES I FIND MYSELF HOPING THAT THE WORST PEOPLE ALIVE ARE ACTUALLY RIGHT. I THINK IT WOULD BE GREAT IF WHAT THESE TERRIBLE PEOPLE ARE SAYING IS TRUE AND IT'S NOT REALLY THAT BAD AFTER ALL AND WE CAN GET BACK TO NORMALCY WITHIN A MONTH OR SO. EVEN THOUGH I KNOW IT'S NOT THE CASE, IT'S LIKE WISHING ON A MONKEY'S PAW THING. I WANT TO GET BACK TO NORMAL, BUT PROVING ALL THESE GHOULS RIGHT IS A BITTER PILL TO SWALLOW.

Totally makes sense. All these people talking about how it's overblown, we can just get back to normal, open things up right now . . . I would love for all of them to be right. They can rub the I told you so's in my face all they want. It would suck, I would fucking hate it, but I would love for them to be right. But the available evidence, and a basic understanding of things, suggests that they're wrong.

THE NARRATIVE THAT THIS IS A PLOT AGAINST TRUMP TO MAKE HIM LOOK BAD ETC. HAS THERE BEEN ANY ATTEMPT ON FOX TO DEAL WITH THE DISSONANCE OF THE QUESTION OF WHY EVERY OTHER COUNTRY IN THE WORLD WOULD BE IN ON A PLOT TO MAKE MR. TRUMP LOOK BAD?

No. Just a hard no there. I hadn't even thought of that until you asked the question. It has not shown up.

DO YOU THINK THE MAJORITY OF PEOPLE ON FOX ARE FUCKING STUPID, EVIL, OR JUST CORRUPT? OR IS IT A COMBINATION OF ALL OF THEM?

That's the timeless question.

DO YOU GIVE ANY CREDENCE TO THE LINE BETWEEN THEIR HARD NEWS AND OPINION SHOWS THAT THEY LIKE TO PLAY UP? IS THAT JUST A CON THEY USE TO THEIR BENEFIT?

It's basically a con. There's no meaningful credence to give it. A straight news show on Fox, you're unlikely to hear anybody call Nancy Pelosi a total dumbass. You're more likely to hear it on the opinion side. But the thrust of the coverage, the thing you're supposed to take away, is wow, Nancy Pelosi is not very good at this. They're all driving to the same point, Fox's news and opinion sides, they're just working at it from a different angle.

WHAT IN YOUR OPINION IS GOING THROUGH THE HEADS OF THE PEOPLE SITTING AT HOME RIGHT NOW WITH FOX NEWS ON IN THE BACKGROUND NINETEEN HOURS A DAY?

Being as charitable to the imaginary Fox News watching everyman as I can, I would guess they probably think social distancing was necessary, it was hard, but we're flattening the curve, and we need to start looking at ending it very soon.

NIGHTMARES ARE DIFFERENT NOW

Nightmares are different now Michelle said when she woke up this morning. While she was sleeping I got into my protective gear and went to Dunkin' Donuts for the first time in a month or so and I got the large iced with milk and one sugar and the medium hot with milk and half of a sugar and I brought it all home and I gave the coffees a bath in the sink a very normal routine when I bring anything home now and I put the Munchkins in a bowl and microwaved them to get the Covid off.

One recurring nightmare I have always had throughout my life is that it's just before a high school football game and I can't find my helmet anywhere no matter how hard I look and everyone is so mad at me and I've let everyone down and weirdly a lot of my old friends tell me they have a very similar dream and anyway someday when this is all over I bet we are all going to have nightmares like that where we find ourselves out in public at say Dunkin' Donuts without our mask and everyone is going to be so mad at us and then we'll wake up and say thank god it was just a dream.

It's April and the mayor of Las Vegas wants to open up the casinos and the hotels as soon as possible. In one of the more let us call it memorable appearances on television in quite some time Carolyn Goodman offered up the citizens of her city as a "control group" to see what happens when all of the expert advice about social distancing is ignored. I suppose taking a gamble like that is appropriate given where she lives. Fuck it why not?

Asked by Anderson Cooper why she was pushing for opening up despite medical guidance she said uh . . . capitalism can defeat the disease (?).

"I am not a private owner. That's the competition in this country, the free enterprise and to be able to make sure that what you offer the public meets the needs of the public," she said. "Right now, we're in a crisis healthwise, and so for a restaurant to be open or a small boutique to be open, they better figure it out. That's their job. That's not the mayor's job."

Later on when Cooper pressed her on whether or not she herself would be down on the casino floors working if they were to reopen she sputtered and deflected before saying "I have a family" that she has to cook for every night so . . . no.

That is of course not just the subtext but now the explicit text of all of these pushes for people to get back to work from Republicans and the so-called "open up" protesters around the country. It's not that they want to get back to work it's that they want other people to get back to working for them and if those people get sick fuck 'em haul in the next batch.

On top of that some of the states like Georgia and Tennessee saying they're going to open back up ASAP are hoping to shift the blame for failing businesses from themselves to the owners. If the government is telling people they can't open and people suffer that is the government's fault but if they say you can open and you still suffer well then that's just the good old-fashioned market at work and it's on you bitches.

I talked to a barista in Las Vegas who told me about working through the early months of the lockdown.

"I work in a Starbucks within a grocery store in Las Vegas, which is not as much on the frontlines as many of the great people I work with, but there is a bizarre level of stress in my head, maybe because of that fact," she said. "Because Starbucks wants to 'reassure' the public we won't close, maybe I should be happy I'm still working (?), yet in my head I get pretty angry thinking about these assholes still coming in and insisting on getting their fancy coffees with their kids more often than not."

"I'm a little embarrassed because I'm not sure my story is important enough. My husband works in one of the higher-end casinos in town. His income is our main income. We have already been kind of tight on money because this job for me is only paying about half of what I used to get. My daughter is still living at home, planning on doing some college courses online. Most of her life is online, but she has good friends and she is a great individual, yet a little sheltered."

"The other day was my daughter's birthday. We had already had to promise her a gift she wanted down the road, because we didn't have the money. And that was the day my husband got the call he was laid off. They were talking April 16 for a return, but I'm not seeing that happen. The casino promised a two week paycheck for everyone, and he got it this past Thursday. The thing is for dealers, the bulk of their income is tips. With the check they sent, they included an average amount of tips into the check, which was greatly appreciated, but we haven't heard any promise of anything since. And my check, well, it's small. They are giving us an extra $2 an hour which brings me to $12.40 an hour—whoo!— but I only work twenty to twenty-five hours a week. The good thing is I do have union health insurance."

"I get more anxiety just watching the wonderful people I work with in the grocery store working fifty-plus hours a week, and certain shelves not being restocked, like paper products and pasta. The store tries to help the workers by keeping some items like water in the back that we can buy after hours, but god, they are working nonstop."

"I have very mixed emotions about even working at this point. I get the grocery store angle, but do these fuckers really need Starbucks? And since we are basically on our own, we have to handle the dirty money, wash our hands, sanitize, then make the drinks. And these fuckers are ordering like three to four drinks at a time, showing up with all their kids. One woman, face mask and gloves, came up to order a drink, then accused me of breathing on the cups after asking me to show her the different sizes. I assured her I would use new cups."

"A random thought: We went shopping today at Walmart. If I'm not infected already I'd be surprised. There are so many people out and about in Las Vegas. I think until someone is affected directly, they don't think it's real."

WE HAVE TO STARVE THE FUCKER

I guess the Trump administration's plan is to hide the bodies and pretend they're not piling up like we did with Iraq?

I briefly convinced myself that there is some number of deaths some horrific massive number with real gravity to it that demands attention and action a tipping point type of number that we might reach whereby Republicans and "open the economy" types might stop acting like they are now. Is it 500,000 I wondered is it a million but if we're being honest no such number likely exists. Instead what will happen is we will come to accept thousands dead every single day as another voice in the churning ambient chorus of suffering we do our best to tune out already much like with gun violence or unnecessary deaths due to the cost of healthcare or the thousands our military kills around the world. Many of us even the "good ones" like me and you already have started to do that in a way right or else how would we manage to function on a daily basis? How do you get up and measure out the coffee and heat up the water and poke your stupid face into the fridge for a nice piece of fruit every morning without pretending if at least for a while that no one is dying outside your walls?

I said this about gun violence back in August of last year in between the shootings in El Paso and Dayton—do you remember which those ones were or did it take a second?—and I suppose it's just what deaths from the pandemic are going to be like going forward.

"It's just like a weather report for a state you don't live in at this point."

Until it happens to you or someone you know and then it's real.

I hit a weird sort of wall the past week where nothing really matters much and nothing brings me any sense of relief or pleasure. I'm not taking any solace from reading or watching TV or drinking or making dinner or sleeping or going for a run or jacking off anymore it's all bountiful and constantly available and so the things we look forward to under normal circumstances have kind of lost their luster. More than usual that is because that's sort of how I've always been as long as you've known me. This has all been like finding a separate basement in your already spooky basement that leads to a sub-subterranean chamber and you're not entirely sure you want to find out what it holds. It's the same way I've always known America was a charnel house of horrors designed to torture the poor but I somehow know that more so than I did in say February. And that's all while living at home farting around on the computer all day so I guess I should shut the fuck up and enjoy my good fortune.

After I wrote that I watched a video of a bunch of people in Florida protesting that they can't go to the gym to exercise by exercising . . . outside of the gym.

They said there was the possibility of a tornado ripping through the state yesterday and I didn't believe it because I've never seen a tornado which means they aren't real. I went about my day with the impotent tornado buzzing around in the back of my mind sowing no destruction and leveling no homes and carried on with my normal routine which is to sit here not thinking about anything besides the one thing we all have to think about.

Does anyone else think about this shit pretty much non-stop and still somehow manage to not actually grasp how much it's going to fuck everything up for years at best and maybe forever?

I read an <u>interview</u> with Werner Herzog just now and the writer goes to him he goes it must be very frustrating to have to isolate like this and Herzog goes:

> "No, I can live with it. Everybody has to live with it and I'm no exception. I do the most aggression against the virus by hunkering down. Which sounds like a paradox, because hunkering down is defensive. But we have to starve the fucker."

Later on last night a bad storm started and I thought maybe tornados are real after all but I was wrong it was just some explosive rain and lightning and thunder and wind and we turned the TV off and watched the lightning and I said wait do you start counting after the lightning strike or the thunder and Michelle said whichever the right one is I already forget and we counted one Mississippi two Mississippi etc. until the storm got closer and then got further away and it was thrilling in a way like we were children how they're bemused by everything in nature how they're experiencing everything for the first time always and I wondered if the rain and the wind and the lightning was destroying anything somewhere else and if it was realer for people other than me for whom it was just a new thing to look at for a while until it was gone and not my problem anymore.

I saw a picture of people spilling out of a bar in San Francisco and a video of a MAGA pud at a crowded bar in Florida saying it's all fake and so on and the president retweeted it and I saw bars packed in Wisconsin and I saw that Texas which opened up a couple weeks ago just had their highest single death total in a day and I read a story in Airmail the newsletter for rich psychos about underground speakeasy clubs in New York City where the invincible and decadent and unbothered youth were dancing and passing around drugs.

"Tequila shots and dry martinis were being passed around, sweaty hand to sweaty hand. Drinks were $10 a pop, cash only. A long-haired man snorted cocaine-and-ketamine swirlies off of mirrored platters lining the sides of a professional D.J. booth. Behind it, a D.J. maneuvered vinyl discs of tech-house records. A good-looking couple passed around props—cowboys hats, studded crowns; I even glimpsed a bright-pink wig—while a brunette girl sat on a floor pillow, licking magic-mushroom chocolate out of an artisanal packet. A supermodel and her boyfriend I recognized from Instagram downed shots—'Cheers to corona!' they said, glasses clinking. Two guys next to me did the elbow bump before laughing and embracing. 'We don't do that!'"

Then I remembered I'd been meaning to get around to rereading *The Masque of the Red Death* by Edgar Allan Poe so I did that just now while the coffee machine was sputtering and whining in the kitchen like it was lonely.

It's the end of May and America is open for business and back to doing what we do best baby and if you need evidence of that look no further than the <u>shooting</u> at a naval base in Texas on Wednesday of this week or the <u>shooting</u> at a mall in Arizona on Thursday. Mercifully no one was killed in either attack I guess our mass shooters are a little rusty like the rest of us but don't worry because the big boys in the government got up to some killing of their own by conducting the first execution of the pandemic. Nature is healing itself.

Walter Barton was put to <u>death</u> on Tuesday for the 1991 killing of a woman named Gladys Kuehler in Ozark, Missouri a crime for which he was tried five times over the decades and for which there was as there often is considerable question about whether or not he actually did.

"Mr. Barton has maintained his innocence since day one; because the case against Mr. Barton was so weak, it took the state five tries to actually convict him and sentence him to death, 'improv[ing its case] time after time because they find more snitches'—and, even then Missouri's highest court affirmed his conviction only by the narrowest of margins, with multiple justices strongly dissenting," the Innocence Project wrote in a request for an independent board to review his conviction.

"His conviction rests entirely upon evidence now known to be two of the leading causes of wrongful conviction:

incentivized jailhouse informant testimony and blood spatter evidence, an infamously unreliable forensic 'science.' Today, there is new, reliable evidence, casting even more doubt on his already troubling conviction. Mr. Barton's case is marred by prosecutorial misconduct, as well as ineffective assistance of counsel, from beginning to end."

"Mr. Barton's case has the hallmarks of a wrongful conviction," they wrote.

I guess they had to take extra precautions for the witnesses to the execution on account of the pandemic. Karen Pojmann a spokeswoman for the Missouri Department of Corrections said they "planned to divide witnesses within three rooms" and that "everyone would be given a temperature check before entering and provided face coverings and hand sanitizer." So that's good. You wouldn't want anyone getting sick at the execution. You wouldn't want them taking anything home with them that they couldn't recover from.

Not too far away from there over the weekend as the Covid death toll odometer inched over 100,000 Missouri was also open for business in its own way with hundreds of revelers packed into a crowded pool bar on the Lake of the Ozarks perhaps silently and invisibly executing each other via partying.

Have you ever been to a pool bar like that they always seem like they're designed by Dante just layers and layers of despair. Speaking of which I watched this movie over the weekend called *Antrum* about a brother and sister who try to find their dead dog by digging a hole to Hell. At the beginning the boy asks his mother if Maxine the dog was in Heaven now and the mother says "No. Because he was bad."

It's not just in places like Missouri that people are itching to get back to business there was a shitty little stunt protest in Brooklyn last week held by people who think getting to the salon is more important than other human lives.

"My fingernails are breaking, I've got hangnails, I've been getting my nails done for 14 years . . . I'm very much into yoga, I can't go to my Bikram yoga studios, I can't go get my eyelashes done, I can't go and socialize with the people that are my friends," a woman from Mississippi named Hillary Angel Barq told *Brooklyn Paper*. "It's led me to depression, it's made me not feel sexual—I mean it's awful."

It does sound awful not going to argue with her there.

Anyway I don't care about that I just wanted an excuse to share this with you the best sentence I've read in all of Covid and maybe all of my life from a story about the protest.

"Frank Scurlock, a former candidate for mayor in New Orleans and heir to an inflatable bounce house fortune, was arrested in 2017 for allegedly masturbating in the backseat of an Uber in California, for which he pled no contest in 2018, according to a report in the *Times-Picayune*."

It's important to keep in mind that the loudest voices when it comes to reopening and getting everyone back to work are usually people like that people who are the heirs to bounce house fortunes and not the actual workers who will be putting their lives at risk at the bounce house factory.

I don't know why people aren't scared to get into a pool with a hundred strangers right now maybe they just love the thrill of gambling. I can personally attest to the high of risking like $50 on a hand of blackjack so can you imagine how much more exciting it must be when you're risking your whole entire life and the lives of everyone around you?

Or maybe a lot of people aren't scared to mingle in the piss and beer water stew literally and metaphorically speaking because our brains have been softened up by too much misinformation just a constant pummeling to the dome every day for years by the news media trustworthy and otherwise. A recent poll by Yahoo News/YouGov for example found that 44% of Republicans believe that "Bill Gates is plotting to use a mass COVID-19 vaccination campaign as a pretext to implant microchips in billions of people and monitor their movements." Democrats are much smarter of course only 19% of them believe that which is . . . uh 1 in 5 Democrats. Not bad!

I don't know why so many people feel the need to divert their very natural and instinctive disdain for the ungodly abomination of billionaires like Gates and George Soros or whoever into believing in made up conspiracies when they could very simply despise them for being billionaires in the first place and doing the actual real life things that billionaires do.

More from the poll:

"The new Yahoo News/YouGov poll found that this 'choose your own reality' effect is distorting perceptions of nearly every aspect of the pandemic, from reopening to vaccination to the official death toll. A broad majority of the public is either 'very' (56 percent) or 'somewhat' concerned (30

percent) about 'false or misleading information being com-
municated about coronavirus.' That sentiment, at least, is not
partisan: More than 80 percent of Democrats, Republicans
and independents agree."

"Yet blame for these concerns varies greatly by political
affiliation. When Democrats are asked to select the top source
of false or misleading information about the coronavirus, 56
percent pick the Trump administration; that number rises to
69 percent among Hillary Clinton voters. Republicans, however, point to the mainstream media (54 percent) as the primary culprit; 61 percent of Trump voters say likewise."

"The result, in many cases, is two different sets of
'facts'—only one of which resembles the truth."

They also found that only half of Americans say they
intend to be vaccinated "if and when a coronavirus vaccine
becomes available." 23% said they will not. Get in the fucking
pool baby.

That film I mentioned *Antrum* comes with a sort of *Blair
Witch/The Ring* style meta framing which I found pretty
corny. The idea is that the actual "film" within the film is so
horrifying that anyone who has ever seen it dies and they
have "experts" and shit talking about it in a fake documen-
tary. I sort of wish they had skipped that and just released
it as is because it's pretty unsettling and gets more so with
each successive layer of Hell the kids dig themselves into. At
a certain point they realize that they've fucked up and might
not be able to turn back at all.

THE MERE ACT OF EXISTING IN THE WORLD

For the first time in as long as I can remember I don't know what to say. Or maybe rather I just don't know where to begin. It's not as if there wasn't always an almost impossible to manage surfeit of bad news to wrestle with before the week when the summer turned but for some reason it feels overwhelming and impenetrable today. How do you poke any air out of a balloon that encompasses the entire world?

That's all particularly true in a week in which we've seen the fallout of the woman who tried to weaponize her whiteness against a Black man in New York City and the murder of George Floyd by the Minneapolis Police Department and the subsequent protests that have been going on in the city for the past couple of days.

Regarding the intersection of the two incidents this week I was reminded of a couple of chapters from my last book.

"When it comes to police violence it's become common to ask ourselves and others: Can you imagine how often these things happened and how little we heard about them before cameras? These encounters happen across America every day. The mere act of existing in the world—taking a nap, barbecuing, moving into an apartment, shopping—is seen as de facto inappropriate when it's being done while Black."

"Of course this is not news. This has not just started happening. What is different is that people have become wise to the fact that sometimes going viral is their only recourse so we are seeing more videos of it posted. And on the plus side many more people do seem to be paying attention to it. Had white Americans listened to people of color talking about their own lived reality for decades they might have understood that this happens all the time. But America at large doesn't tend to do that. Even with the rise of the Black Lives Matter movement there will remain a steadfast and indignant percentage of people—even when given clear evidence of actual crimes, even cold-blooded murder being carried out by police—insisting on seeing all the evidence, or those who wonder what the obviously-guilty Black man must have done to provoke the righteous police into killing him. They always have it coming."

I was frustrated being unable to see and learn exactly what was going on in Minneapolis sitting here on my ass in my home in Massachusetts the past two nights so I talked to two people who were on the scene to explain what they saw and what it feels like in the city of Minneapolis right now.

The first is a young activist named David Gilbert-Pederson.

WHAT WAS YOUR EXPERIENCE OVER THE PAST COUPLE DAYS?

I went down to the protest at 38th and Chicago on Tuesday where brother George Floyd was killed. What we saw at the beginning of that gathering was probably the most beautiful and effective implementation of mutual aid since the beginning of Covid. We saw local distilleries bringing out bottles of hand sanitizer to hand out to crowds. People were handing out free gloves, free masks, bottles of water, giving people sanitizer to take home to their families. It was a beautiful sign of mutual aid and solidarity in the city.

I didn't really know what the plan was when we left 38th and Chicago, where the route was going, but we started walking down 38th, a pretty major thoroughfare, and folks were lining the street, coming out of their houses. There wasn't a cop in sight anywhere on the march. When we got to the precinct there were no police there at first. Then some windows were broken and the police erupted out of the building shooting tear gas and those marking canisters, rubber bullets, flash-bangs. I was standing in a crowd of mostly teenagers that were getting hit hard by the tear gas and rubber bullets. People had started to run when the tear gas happened, and I was trying to tell people to slow down so they don't get trampled. I was talking to a pretty big group of young folks, and I said anyone who has paint on them from those marking canisters has to wash it off right now. I leaned down to pour some water on this young woman's eyes and immediately got hit in the thigh with a rubber bullet. I looked down and felt explosive pain in my thigh. I didn't see any paint, so I had this panic moment of "did I just get shot?"

SO IT TOOK YOU A MINUTE TO REALIZE WHAT HAPPENED?

Yeah. I fell to the ground and was grabbing my leg. People came over to ask me if I was ok. I was able to get up and I ran.

So we pulled back to a hill . . . but then tear gas hit us again. People scattered across Highway 55. There were people that almost got hit by cars. People were getting trampled. One of the people I was with ran into a road sign because vision was super impaired from all the gas being used. People were running through the neighborhoods and for about a mile away there was still tear gas in the air.

WERE PEOPLE SCARED OR ANGRY?

A lot of folks were scared. A lot of people were really upset and angry. There was one older woman in her sixties or seventies crying, screaming for her son she couldn't find. There were these three Somali girls looking for their older brother. There was a group of some older folks more experienced with protests helping people get medical attention. Again, what we saw in that moment was a beautiful solidarity. We saw people running away from tear gas in this panic, and people would scream we need milk over here or water or Maalox or whatever people had. People talk about a fucking riot, but what we saw was our community coming together and standing in solidarity, even in this terrifying moment. Us being able to build a community outside of the confines of what capitalism and imperialism and militarism have taught us and ingrained in us to believe is true. The city didn't do mutual aid in the way that happened at 38th and Chicago. The police weren't administering first aid in the way people were administering it to each other up on that freeway.

I'M SURE IT'S INSPIRING TO SEE. WHAT IS THE GENERAL FEELING RIGHT NOW FROM PEOPLE YOU ARE TALKING TO? WHAT DO YOU ALL WANT TO SEE COME OUT OF THIS?

We have to see these officers arrested and charged. They got fired and that's great, but we need to see them criminally charged. And we need to see some leadership from our elected officials and our police chief. You write about police violence so you understand, but the Abuka Sanders case that happened in the early 2000s, Courtney Williams, a fifteen-year-old kid shot by the Minneapolis police, Terrence Franklin, Jamar Clark, Philando Castile . . . the state and the metro is just kind of rife with anger and tension. People haven't seen justice served. There has been a high profile murder of an unarmed person in the city at least every year since 2010 . . . We have one of the highest disparities of shootings of unarmed people when it comes to the Black and white disparity. People are just angry. They're just done. What they got told was, oh, we need to enact stronger laws, or we need to change the mayor, or the council. But what we've seen is no substantive change. I grew up maybe about two miles from the 3rd Precinct. People are just so angry and feel so hopeless about the situation with the police. They feel so much like the police could kill them or their family or friend at any moment. Whatever legitimate violence there was last night, outside of agent provocateurs, was just a reflection of people's deep, deep anger and yearning for justice.

WHAT HAPPENS WITH THESE SITUATIONS EVERY TIME IS ALREADY HAPPENING, THE SHITTY PEOPLE ARE GOING TO FOCUS ON BUILDINGS BEING BURNED, AND THE POOR TARGET AND ALL THAT. THAT'S GOT TO BE REALLY INFURIATING, TO SEE THE NARRATIVE SWITCH TO THAT, BY PEOPLE WHO DON'T ACTUALLY GIVE A SHIT ABOUT HUMAN LIFE. DID YOU SEE ANYTHING, OR SUSPECT OUTSIDE PEOPLE OF STARTING SHIT?

Right. There's a video that shows someone really sketchy starting a fire at Auto Zone people are sharing on Twitter. I know there's stuff like that. But I also know there are a lot of people that are just traumatized and hurt and scared. When the institutions fail us, even though we know that they don't protect us . . . The video [of Floyd's murder] was just so callous and egregious. And the time it's taking the officers to get charged has led to this boiling point. I don't want to speak on people's intentions, but what we saw was an explosion of anger about a system that's killed hundreds of people in our state and thousands in our country. I just feel like this is the byproduct of so many years of impunity.

THERE WERE TWO MAJOR THINGS THIS WEEK IN THE NEWS, THE LADY IN NEW YORK THREATENING TO CALL THE POLICE, AND GEORGE FLOYD'S KILLING. HAVE YOU THOUGHT ABOUT HOW THIS KILLING ILLUSTRATES EXACTLY WHAT THE PROBLEM WAS WITH WHAT SHE WAS TRYING TO DO THERE?

Absolutely. We had this happen two nights ago, a rich white man in his office building, when two young Black entrepreneurs were using the gym at the building, he called the cops on them, and he ended up losing his lease in the building. Really what we're seeing is that people are now weaponizing the police against Black and Brown people. But in targeted ways. It's not just a systemic thing, it's almost like swatting. Maybe they don't realize the gravity of the situation, but that's inexcusable. If you turn on the news you're going to see a story of Black people killed. Even the last few months: Breonna Taylor, Ahmaud Arbery . . . If you're willing to weaponize the police against other people like this . . . It's really just a weaponization of whiteness against Black people. What we're seeing is that people are starting to record this stuff. These are consistent problems that have festered, but motherfuckers now have ways to document it. And with the variety of videos and the heightened state of awareness these stories spread.

I FEEL LIKE THERE WAS A SWITCH A COUPLE YEARS AGO. PEOPLE HAVE BEEN FILMING POLICE VIOLENCE, AND EVERYONE GETS UPSET ABOUT THAT, BUT THE PAST COUPLE YEARS PEOPLE HAVE STARTED FILMING MORE "MINOR" AGGRESSIONS IN A WAY. WE DON'T HAVE TO SEE SOMEONE BE KILLED TO BE UPSET, NOW WE SEE THE STEPS THAT HAPPENED BEFORE . . .

Yes, what happens before somebody dies.

Derek is another protestor who was on hand last night and says he got hit by a tear gas canister.

SO WHAT HAPPENED LAST NIGHT?

In the beginning we were surrounding the precinct, which is across the street from the Target. They just started firing round after round of tear gas. They were pretty much pushing us toward the back [toward the stores]. It was just a matter of time before shit got smashed up. They were fucking firing man, it was terrifying.

YOU GOT HIT?

Yeah. We were at the frontline on another block, and they had their horses behind them, and all of a sudden everybody started running. I see this guy fall on his bike and as I'm helping him up I feel my shoulder get hit. I couldn't breathe because it was a chemical agent they shot me with. I got helped by street medics. They were really organized. It was great that they were there. The police turned it into a war zone.

ARE YOU STILL IN PAIN?

Absolutely. My arm is still pretty fucked up. I'm kind of shell-shocked honestly.

WERE THE POLICE GIVING ORDERS TO DISPERSE OR ANYTHING?

They didn't say shit. They were silent. They pretty much just had smirks on their faces. When we were chanting and getting really revved up, all of a sudden it would be like: *bang bang*! We'd run back, then move back to our position. They didn't say anything.

HAVE YOU EVER SEEN ANYTHING LIKE THIS?

Never. I think this is history.

WHAT'S THE CITY LIKE THIS MORNING?

I can hear helicopters, sirens everywhere. The street that was hit, Lake Street, it looks like a warzone. Glass, gas canisters. Everything is on fire. They're still putting it out.

DO YOU EXPECT ANYTHING ELSE TO HAPPEN TODAY?

If there is something tonight it's going to look a lot different. Probably a hell of a lot more militant and potentially more deadly. I think people will also come prepared to meet that. It's scary to think.

DO YOU FEEL UNSAFE IN GENERAL AROUND THE CITY AS A BLACK MAN?

Absolutely. The cops in Minneapolis are just terrorists. They killed Philando in cold blood. Jamar Clark. Now George Floyd. People don't think of Minnesota and Minneapolis as a place like that, but it's worse than a lot of other places. We have terrible amounts of disparity. It's really fucked up. They have free reign. The city is afraid of the police chief Bob Kroll.

DO YOU THINK PEOPLE DON'T UNDERSTAND WHAT MINNEAPOLIS IS AROUND THE COUNTRY?

I think it's hard to understand. The media portrayal doesn't cover it, but we have a giant unhoused indigenous population living in tents. This is Dakota land after all. And so they've just been terribly oppressed. And Black folks here have it terrible as well. In Minneapolis I think Black folks are like thirteen times more likely to be killed by police.

PUTTING ON YOUR MOST OPTIMISTIC HAT, WHICH IS OBVIOUSLY HARD TO DO, WHAT HOPE DO YOU HAVE FOR SOMETHING THAT MIGHT COME OUT

OF THIS?

I hope for one Minneapolis understands that they can't do this to us anymore. I hope that we get organized, and that we can defund the Minneapolis Police Department. I hope that everyone remembers the names of George Floyd, Jamar Clark, and Philando Castile forever. People need to know what's going.

WHAT'S YOUR REACTION TO HOW THE COP KISSERS ARE RIGHT NOW TURNING THIS INTO A STORY ABOUT LOOTING AND SHIT?

My response to that is that they knew and they set it up to happen. As they were pushing us back, they were pushing us back into these positions where the only cover was those buildings. The opportunity presented itself and shit got chaotic. I think they fully intended it to happen. When you're being shelled repeatedly with rubber bullets and tear gas you don't have many options.

THEY WOULD PREFER THAT YOU VOTE THE POLICE BATON OFF OF YOUR SKULL

It's May and George Floyd has been killed by the police in Minneapolis. It's March and Breonna Taylor has been killed by police in Louisville. It's August and Jacob Blake has been shot and seriously injured by police in Kenosha.

Remember like two months in when we are all desperate for a break from the monotony?

It's too much now man. It is overwhelming. I am at long last overwhelmed. In any normal week any one of a thousand things we've all seen happen in just the past two days of the uprising would have been enough to write five thousand words about but how does one go about choosing among them right now? How do you pick one instance of unchecked state violence against the citizenry as an entry point? Presenting one as the singular overarching example to stand in for the whole would be woefully inadequate. It would feel like an insult to all the ones you left out.

Just now I turned on the cable news like a fucking idiot and watched I don't know let's say it was a tanker truck plowing through a crowd of a thousand people marching along a highway in Minneapolis that was supposed to have been shut down. Maybe it was police in New York or Los

Angeles attempting to run over protestors a technique that has become something of a pattern in law enforcement of late in cities around the country.

While I was watching I felt this dark ink creeping through my skin and I felt my chest getting heavy and it wasn't until after about an hour of that feeling of my body resetting to its newly natural equilibrium of agitation and exhaustion—I feel always like I've got an IV of adrenaline in one arm and an IV of anesthesia in the other—that I recognized that the feeling had gone away for a merciful few hours earlier. I had been back in Boston this week marching and protesting and chanting and silently kneeling and communing together with my fellow citizens of Massachusetts who like people everywhere else have had enough. For a few hours each time I found solace in solidarity and I can't overstate how freeing that was. An unburdening.

Of course things would become more confrontational in Boston on a few nights early on much like in every other city but there's righteousness to be found in that as well. Who gives a fuck about a store window?

Boston's mayor sent out some platitudes about respecting our rights to assemble and have our voices heard and get our asses kicked by his fucking goons but there was one thing he said which almost all politicians and liberals and conservatives alike who are uncomfortable with disorder are saying which is that he blamed any violence on people from "outside the city" and that sort of thing has really angered me of late in part because why wouldn't people who aren't technically residents of a major metropolitan area travel there to protest? The idea that you have to be an authorized resident of a city to go to a protest there is so fucking infuriating to me. I'm not talking about "destroying" the city but protesting there. Police hurt us everywhere but mostly in the big cities so it makes sense to me that that's where we would go to demand they stop. Especially when it's the state capitals where our governments are located.

More than that though this idea has taken root everywhere that in every city there are paid crisis actors and people being "bussed in" to cause damage and that is meant to do a few things one of which is to forestall any sense of rising solidarity among the different groups protesting the use of state violence against citizens and disproportionately against people of color.

The second thing is it's an attempt to create an "out group" that does not fall under the jurisdiction of our leaders. If a mayor or governor says the people causing trouble aren't his or her people it's some other "foreign" group then anything they say or do can be dismissed as illegitimate. Those people are not my people and therefore what they are asking for is not my responsibility to fix.

Thirdly it's ah fuck I forgot the third one. Gonna be honest with you guys I have not exactly been practicing self-care vis-à-vis the old mental health and substance use over here. I've been lashing out at friends and being cruel and spoiling for a fight with anyone who moderately disappoints me and I'm sorry about that. Shit what was I going to say . . .

In any case please shut the fuck up about outside agitators unless you mean the police very few of whom even live in the cities they menace.

Yes there are some small percentage of "fake protestors" just as there are (being very very generous here) a handful of decent human-being cops. But if you're talking about either right now you're obfuscating the actual problem. Are there white supremacists in our midst wreaking havoc? Sure. Are there some people destroying things for fun? Maybe. But it does not matter. Police brutalize and murder people every single day. They are doing it right now. They're doing it more than ever right now. That's the issue. Anything else you're talking about is an attempt to distract from that.

Another means of distraction people seem to be really invested in lately is sharing stories of friendly cops here and there kneeling and marching and not killing people for five minutes like it's a video of a bear getting into someone's swimming pool. Awwww that's not what they're supposed to do! He thinks he's people. So to that end I'm begging you other white people especially not to share feel good pictures of cops meeting the baseline expected standards of human decency and professionalism. It's no different than writing "not all cops" which is a synonym for "all lives matter" which is another way of saying "I am fine with systemic racism and police brutality."

Oh right I remembered the third thing.

Picking out various groups amidst the protests who are really responsible for the destruction and don't have their official protest papers in order is a way—especially for comfortable white libs—to disprove of the protest in more socially respectable terms. None of them would dare speak up against people of color protesting for their lives but they also really really don't like the idea of people pushing back against the state and forcing change—they would prefer that you vote the police baton off of your skull — so they take that instinctual discomfort they are feeling and place it upon a more socially acceptable group to despise which is as it always is the left.

That's why in particular cable news libs are so fucking horny to have Antifa or whatever to be mad at now they just constitutionally cannot level criticism at the police or Black folks on air it's abhorrent to them. The two guiding principles of the lib mind are you can't blame anything on people of color because being perceived as racist is social and professional death and you also can't criticize the people whose job it is to oppress them because being perceived as anti-police makes you some kind of activist. You can be against some specific police but not The Police. Due to "journalism" taking a stance against the police on a systemic and not merely "a few bad apples" level is seen as being biased and unobjective just like when it comes to criticizing the military.

That's also true of Democrat politicians approximately zero of whom I've seen use the actual words systemic police brutality or talked about how to fix this in any way besides soggy broad messages of healing and coming together. Democrat politicians prefer to call out generic racism as the problem because it's amorphous and uncontainable and not the specific ingrained racism of police forces which they actually have power over and would then have to put their necks out to stop.

I WANT TO HUG EVERYONE
I KNOW

It's June and one thing I would like to see come out of all this besides all the other necessary things is for media to please stop considering the police a reliable source when reporting on activities they themselves are a party to. Journalists are petrified of writing that anything happened without an official government account giving them permission because they think that provides them cover if it turns out to be a lie. But with cops it almost always is a lie. Police lie. Say that to yourself. Remember it.

When someone is arrested reporters might get a statement from them or their lawyer but it's considered de facto suspicious because they're clearly biased whereas the cops' statement is much more heavily weighted and the similar bias is ignored.

This is why I always say the media consider themselves a deputized branch of the police. And for nothing but deference to power! They get nothing out of it and the rest of us in the public and in particular the ones being brutalized suffer for it.

The rules of objectivity in journalism are fake. People literally just made them up! They aren't the laws of physics. You're already failing your dumb frat pledge honor code of objectivity by trusting the cops so there's no reason why you can't adjust the dial to always start trusting the people being harmed by state violence.

Not that it matters I guess. There isn't going to be any media left besides like five giant corporations soon so who cares.

I marched again in Boston this weekend peacefully and without much of note to report besides a rising sense of solidarity. The eeriness of a city being largely empty and yet filled with activity all pointed in one direction was unsettling like well I keep wanting to say everything is like something from a film but it's not films are like something from life. Had I known I was going to have to commute regularly to my new job at the protest factory I might've picked a place to live closer to the city. It's hard to report on a march while you're in the midst of it because it feels so massive and bigger than you and it's more than any individual that makes up a piece of the whole. You can talk to a person but you can't interview a crowd and in any case for a couple of weeks I wanted to stop being a reporter and just be there to take part.

It's really weird to bump into people at a march when we're all wearing masks by the way. People you're very happy to see but you can't get too close to them or hug them or even give a fist bump. I want to hug everyone I know and tell them everything is going to get better but I don't know that I could say so earnestly. I guess since I'm wearing a mask they wouldn't be able to read my face and know that I was lying.

Mostly at every march I've been to I've stayed to the side not in the thick of the crowd walking along at a slight remove. To be honest I'm kind of scared of catching Covid at one of these things.

On Monday we went to a protest at the Robbins House a "historic early 19th century house formerly inhabited by the first generation of descendants of formerly enslaved African American Revolutionary War veteran Caesar Robbins and by fugitive slave Jack Garrison." It was . . . nice and well-meaning but also sort of weird due to it's in Concord which is one of the richest towns in all of Massachusetts with about a 2% African American population. To get there we had to cross the highway on some literal "other side of the tracks" shit from our modest town and we almost crashed like five times from gawking at all the mansions that line the streets. Is that a house or an entire Colonial-ass looking hotel I asked like five times.

One of the speakers drew parallels between the situation today and Tulsa's "Black Wall Street" massacre. A number of Black folks from the local community spoke and some of them were powerful and stirring and then they opened it up to everyone and there were a lot of earnest speeches from white people but then a little girl came up and started talking about her coloring book and making the people Black and some other woman chided people for beef on the local town Facebook page which was funny to see at a time like this but I believed her because local town Facebook pages are basically Klan rallies and then the cop chief came up and said some shit about disavowing the tactics used on George Floyd but you could tell he was sort of lying because cops cannot

speak without lying. Then I had to leave before I did something stupid like go up there and get myself into trouble.

So then we walked across the street to the Old North
Bridge the spot where the first American militiamen—organized protests!—got their shit together to fight back against
the British and I thought this is a great place to be right now
how moving and powerful and shit and I thought mostly that
I could probably go for a really nice jog around here.

Then the next night I went to another suburban protest
nearby and another and they kept going for days around here
just hundreds and hundreds of largely white suburban kids
shouting and yelling and waving signs all in their masks and
it was something like inspiring. It was all miles away from
the cities where police are their worst but something had
broken open in the country and the people who generally
don't have to worry about police violence themselves had
decided to make it their problem now too.

Not long after that on a Tuesday evening in the first
week of June Donald Trump ordered the area outside the
White House cleared of protesters by law enforcement who
used tear gas and flash-bang grenades to dispel the crowd.
The impetus was a staged photo opportunity in front of the
historic St. John's Episcopal Church, which was quickly con-
demned by religious leaders.

"Let me be clear, the president just used a Bible, the most
sacred text of the Judeo-Christian tradition, and one of the
churches of my diocese, without permission, as a backdrop
for a message antithetical to the teachings of Jesus," The Right

Rev Mariann Budde, the Episcopal bishop of Washington, told the *Washington Post*.

Asked by a reporter if the prop was *his* Bible, Trump responded: "It's a Bible."

It's September and I just saw a story that the Department of Defense's lead military officer in D.C. considered using a fucking heat ray against protestors the day he did his little stunt. In a discussion about whether or not to use it the military guys noted the weapon "can provide our troops a capability they currently do not have, the ability to reach out and engage potential adversaries at distances well beyond small arms range, and in a safe, effective, and non-lethal manner" by providing "a sensation of intense heat on the surface of the skin. The effect is overwhelming, causing an immediate repel response by the targeted individual."

Previously our government had considered using the skin-cooking laser on migrants at the border in the lead up to the 2018 midterms.

It's weird isn't it that it occurs to us that the government microwaving citizens is somehow so much worse than just breaking their skulls and bones or blasting them with poison gas or shooting bullets at them but I suppose it is because it seems new and novel. Maybe someday it will seem old hat. Everything that is bad and new seems a worse type of bad and then once it becomes merely bad and old it's easier to accept and that applies to types of state violence and also every single other thing done by this administration in general.

WE JUST WANT TO GET PEOPLE OUT

"Immigrants detained at the La Palma Correctional Center near Eloy have become increasingly desperate as the new coronavirus outbreak at the facility has grown into to one of the biggest in the nation," the *Arizona Republic* reported at the beginning of June. Seventy-six of the undocumented immigrants being imprisoned there had tested positive for the virus, making it the sixth-largest outbreak in the country at the time.

Like at many of the other facilities across the country people being detained there said they had been afforded inadequate opportunity to practice proper hygiene or to socially distance from one another.

"Their letters tell me that they are very concerned and they are very desperate to either get out or get medical attention," Jill Japan a woman corresponding with two detainees told the paper. "And they are concerned that if they get sick they won't be attended to. They are afraid they are going to die."

That came as yet another hunger strike protesting such conditions began at the Northwest Detention Center in Tacoma, Washington.

"Despite clear medical evidence of the highly contagious nature of COVID-19, ICE continues to transfer people detained in its hundreds of facilities across the country to and from detention centers with massive COVID-19 breakouts," according to the advocacy group La Resistencia.

Since the outbreak of the pandemic there have been at least twenty hunger strikes by at least 2,000 detainees in ten states around the country according to the Detention Watch Network. As of June at least two immigrants had died from Covid-related complications while in custody, while a third died shortly after being released. A fourth died of suicide after repeatedly requesting release due to complicating medical conditions. As of August seventeen had died in custody in the fiscal year. Since 2003, 211 people have died in ICE immigrant detention.

In early June numerous immigrant and undocumented advocacy groups took part in a national day of action to #freethemall with protests inside and outside of the detention centers.

That week I spoke with Setareh Ghandehari, the Advocacy Manager of Detention Watch Network about conditions for detained migrants under the pandemic.

MAYBE IT'S JUST ME, BUT MY IMPRESSION IS IT SEEMS LIKE A LOT OF THE ATTENTION THAT WAS BEING PAID TO THE CONDITIONS WE'RE SUBJECTING MIGRANTS TO IN DETENTION DISAPPEARED WITH THE ARRIVAL OF THE PANDEMIC. IS THAT FAIR TO SAY?

I think that's fair. At least in the beginning. It's the news cycle, right? The pandemic took over everything. Even the election. We've been seeing a lot of activity from grassroots organizations for people in detention, and it's not being covered to the extent we would like to see, but I think there's a lot happening in terms of people speaking out about it. There has been some coverage but that could also just be that's where my focus is.

BROADLY SPEAKING WHAT HAS TRANSPIRED FOR PEOPLE IN DETENTION IN THE PAST FEW MONTHS? HAVE THINGS GOTTEN MUCH WORSE, OR HAS IT REMAINED LARGELY THE SAME?

The pandemic has really magnified the situation in immigration detention. As with a lot of things in society it's laid bare the serious and systemic flaws. I would say things have changed in the sense that . . . I don't want to say the stakes are higher, the stakes have always been high, it's always been life or death. But when you have a pandemic, the fact that ICE has a history of medical neglect, a history of not having adequate access to soap and hygiene, the fact that people are not able to socially distance, which has not changed, all these things that are historically true make the situation that much worse when you're dealing with a rapidly spreading virus. Once it starts spreading, if people aren't provided with soap, and can't socially distance, and don't have masks and gloves, it becomes a very tragic situation.

IT SEEMS LIKE IT WAS ALREADY A NIGHTMARE OF NEGLECT AND ABUSE TO BEGIN WITH. ADDING IN THIS CONTAGIOUS DEADLY DISEASE MUST HAVE EXACERBATED THINGS TERRIBLY.

Yes. In 2018 there was an outbreak of mumps. That outbreak spread rapidly because of the way ICE responded, so we know they don't know how to respond to infectious disease outbreaks. That was mumps, something we know how to deal with. If they couldn't handle that, what's the hope of them acting appropriately now?

DO YOU HAVE A SENSE OF HOW MANY DEATHS AND CASES OF COVID HAVE BEEN REPORTED IN THE FACILITIES?

ICE reports on the number of people that have been confirmed to have the virus they've tested. Right now it's something like almost 26,000 people in detention at this moment. They've tested a little more than 2,670 last I checked. 1,392 are confirmed with Covid. That's only the people they've tested. There are people who should be tested that aren't being tested. We can assume the number is much higher than what they're reporting.

DO YOU BELIEVE THEM? I DON'T, BUT WHAT DOES YOUR GROUP THINK?

No. We don't trust them for anything. Is it true that they've tested 2,670 people? Maybe. Is it true that of those people 1,392 are confirmed? Probably. But do we trust that everyone who needs a test is getting a test? No. It's a mixed bag. The numbers are useful in that it gives us a sense of the rate of infection. If 50 percent of the people being tested are infected, I think it helps us understand how grave the situation is because we know the numbers are likely higher. There have been people complaining about symptoms that don't get tested, they have fever, or difficulty breathing . . . How they decide who gets tested I couldn't tell you.

THERE HAVE BEEN A COUPLE OF CONFIRMED DEATHS?

Since the outbreak there have been two confirmed deaths of people who died of Covid-related symptoms while they were in custody. One person died right after being released of Covid-related complications, so he almost certainly contracted while he was in detention, and they released him, and he died shortly after. There was a fourth person who died by suicide, who several times had requested release because he had several risk factors that made him at risk.

TERRIBLE. WHAT SORTS OF PROTESTS ARE YOU GUYS SEEING INSIDE AND OUTSIDE OF THE FACILITIES?

I think that's really significant. Since March we've recorded at least twenty hunger strikes within facilities across the country. Something like 2,000 people have been participating in ten different states. For reference, in all of 2019 there were thirteen hunger strikes. They're really taking huge risks. The way that ICE has been responding has been retaliating by putting people in solitary, barring them from contacting counsel. This terrible irony, when they're going on hunger strike for fear of their lives, they're being denied medical attention. We've also heard of work stoppages. People are using different ways of getting their voices heard.

In terms of organizing on the outside we've seen a lot of car rallies. People showing up outside detention centers to show support and make sure people inside know they're being supported. We've people who have relationships with people inside sharing out their demands. Yesterday we had a national day of action.

WHAT OVERLAPS ARE YOU SEEING BETWEEN THE WAYS IMMIGRANTS ARE TREATED AND SOME OF THE UPRISINGS WE'RE SEEING AROUND THE COUNTRY RIGHT NOW IN RESPONSE TO POLICE VIOLENCE? IS THERE A CONNECTIVE TISSUE THERE?

I think so. It's racism against Black and Brown folks and the criminalization of immigrants is part of this overall racist system. It's the same struggle against racism and xenophobia and mass incarceration. We see immigration detention as an extension of the criminalization of Black and Brown bodies. The profit incentive around putting Black and Brown bodies in jail and cages, it's really related in that sense. On top of that we see the criminal system is also a pipeline into the immigration detention system, so we see them as very connected and part of the same struggle.

WHAT ARE A COUPLE ACTIONS YOU ARE RECOMMENDING THAT PEOPLE WHO ARE CONCERNED ABOUT THIS CAN TAKE? IT CAN FEEL OVERWHELMING AND ONE MIGHT FEEL HELPLESS. THOSE OF US WHO ARE COMFORTABLE MIGHT BE TEMPTED TO STICK OUR HEADS IN THE SAND.

Obviously the easy one is sign a petition and share it to your people. How much are petitions worth, but it can be a spark for a conversation with your family and friends. That's an easy one. We have a Free Them All petition on MoveOn.org. We're calling for ICE to release everyone. They have the discretion to do so, so if they wanted to they could. In terms of other concrete actions, you can contact ICE, your local field office directors. And we especially want people to contact their elected officials and ask them to contact their local ICE field directors. ICE has offices all across the country and they have a lot of discretion about who they keep in detention and who they release. We're trying to build up pressure to get people released at that level.

The other thing I would say is to get in touch with local groups organizing in your area. There are groups across the country doing this work, so get in touch with them, see how you can get involved. We're happy to put people in touch if you can't figure out who those groups are. It's especially important to follow the lead of immigrant-led groups doing this work.

The other thing I would say is donate to bail funds. That's another similarity with the criminal justice movement. We just want to get people out. We want everyone out without strings attached, but sometimes the practicality is someone's been offered the opportunity to get out on bond, and they need money to pay it.

I THINK THEY DO IT BECAUSE THEY GET AWAY WITH IT

It's June and a judge in New York has denied a lawsuit brought by the Legal Aid Society against the NYPD on behalf of over a hundred people being detained illegally for days at a time in violation of the state's twenty-four-hour arrest-to-arraignment requirement.

Typically people arrested at protests will be given a summons or desk appearance ticket and not be detained but Supreme Court Justice James Burke said the extraordinary circumstances of a pandemic and mass protests—"a crisis within a crisis"—have slowed things down. The Legal Aid Society and others argued that the decision is a means of further punishing protestors who are being unnecessarily held in crowded and unsafe conditions during the pandemic.

"The police department has a history . . . of deliberately delaying people's arraignments because they don't like what they're doing on the street," said the Legal Aid Society's Russell Novack.

I spoke with Emma Goodman, an attorney in the Special Litigation Unit at the Legal Aid Society, about why this is such a serious violation of citizens' rights and about how much the cops fucking suck.

CAN YOU EXPLAIN THE SITUATION FOR PEOPLE WHO HAVEN'T BEEN FOLLOWING THIS CASE?

In New York there was a case decided in the 1990s that our office filed that made it illegal for them to hold people from arrest to arraignment for more than twenty-four hours.

THAT'S _ROUNDTREE_?

Yes. That was back in 1991. What's happening is that they're holding people for days on end. So they're just violating _Roundtree_ very clearly. Most of the people that are being held are being held for non-violent felonies. So what they've done—there's no looting statute in New York—so they've charged people with non-violent burglary charges. Those charges allow people to be held in until arraignment, but then once they actually get to see a judge they will all be released. The judge can't hold them in.

BUT THEY'RE DOING THAT ANYWAY NOW?

They're doing it because they're not letting them get arraigned. The delay from when they're arrested to when they actually see a judge is way more than twenty-four hours. Some people have been held for three or four days.

IS THIS JUST IN THE PAST WEEK, OR HAS IT BEEN GOING ON FOR A WHILE?

It being hundreds of people in the system has just been in the past week. There have always been issues here and there, and we file individual writs, but the reason we did a mass writ is because there were about 400 people in the system waiting to see a judge.

THE JUDGE SAID SOMETHING WEIRD ABOUT USING THE PANDEMIC TO JUSTIFY IT. ISN'T THAT . . . COUNTERINTUITIVE?

It was pretty incredible. Judge Burke, to give you a little background, he was just overturned yesterday on a case where he had refused to let defense counsel question a cop about prior misconduct cases against him. So that tells you a little bit about where his leanings are.

A COP-LOVING JUDGE.

Former prosecutor. Likes the cops. Likes the DAs.

SO DO YOU THINK THIS IS A SPITEFUL PUNITIVE DECISION?

I think so. Especially because to me it seems like the law is so clear that people are being held for more than twenty-four hours, and there's no way the NYPD and the courts have figured out how to avoid that. Also, all of these people will get out once they see a judge. It's not like you're letting people out that would otherwise be held in on bail indefinitely. You can't be held on bail in these cases. So it's just making people suffer for several more days while the NYPD delays paperwork, and makes people suffer because they're protesting.

I'M NOT A LAWYER BUT I FEEL LIKE VIOLATING HABEAS CORPUS IS A PRETTY BIG DEAL!

That's what we filed, a writ of habeas corpus, which the judge denied. I think we'll file a notice of appeal today and we'll see where it goes. One of the things that's interesting is we filed the writ a couple days ago and immediately they started moving people along more quickly. When we first filed just in Manhattan there were more than 200 people that were sitting and waiting to be arraigned. As of this morning it's down to 80 people.

HAVE YOU HEARD STORIES FROM PEOPLE BEING HELD ABOUT THE CONDITIONS?

They're pretty awful. When people are being held before arraignment, because it's supposed to be less than twenty-four hours, it's not like you're taken somewhere with beds and a comfortable place to rest. You're held in a cell with dozens of other people. The NYPD yesterday were trying to make their case why they couldn't do this more quickly, but essentially admitted the conditions were horrible to the judge. That's another potential lawsuit on a separate issue about the conditions.

One of the holding areas where they take men in Manhattan holds up to 150 people. There's one toilet. There is running water but no hand sanitizer. They took that away because they said people were making weapons out of the containers. There are benches but no beds. They're just being held there indefinitely. Our clients are telling us there's one toilet, and it's backed up and overflowing. It smells horrible.

THIS IS PUTTING PEOPLE'S LIVES AT FURTHER RISK FOR THE VIRUS.

Going back to what you said about the judge's decision, it never ceases to amaze me the logic that people who hate our clients come up with to punish them further. So he's saying because of the pandemic we should hold people in indefinitely, when that's exactly why you should be releasing people.

IT SEEMS LIKE THE NYPD HAVE TAKEN OVER THE CITY AND ARE JUST TAKING OUT VENGEANCE ON PEOPLE.

That's definitely how it feels. We're seeing them pull out everything from the old police beating down protest playbook from over the decades. They did the same thing where they just held people for days on end after the 2004 Republican convention. They rounded up thousands of people and just held them. They said it was an emergency. But they were just sitting on the paperwork. They weren't trying to process them because they didn't like that they were protesting Republicans. It was very obvious what was happening. That's part of the NYPD playbook we're seeing here.

Another thing they appear to be doing is moving people around between different boroughs. I don't know if it's for the same reasons they did it in the past, but in the past they did it, before this *Roundtree* habeas corpus case, to fudge the numbers to make it look like people weren't being held for more than twenty-four hours. Very suspicious they've started doing that after we filed our writ.

Two big things that are very concerning to us are that the people who were part of our writ were people who were actually arrested. But there are a few different ways the police can process somebody where they're not officially arrested. The point is they're supposed to get a summons or a desk arrest ticket to return to court on your own in a couple months. What they're doing is they're holding all of those people that are just supposed to be issued a ticket for some period of time in some centralized location. They say they can't issue tickets on the street because there's too many pro-testers, which is just illegal detention.

IT'S REALLY ALARMING HOW TENUOUS THIS STUFF ALL SEEMS TO BE AND HOW QUICKLY IT'S FALLING APART. ARE YOU ALARMED?

Yes and no. I'm alarmed by what they're doing. I'm not sur-prised by it. All the injustices people are seeing in the news are things that I've witnessed constantly in my career. It's why I've always hated the NYPD. This is how they act. It used to be something people didn't know about, so it's an interest-ing time to be doing this kind of work and to be in the com-munities that have always been advocating for change. On the one hand it's horrible, of course, but on the other hand everyone is seeing it for what it truly is. That's a big deal. It's actually very exciting too. Everybody, kind of the nice liberal but I still like the cops people, are finally seeing what's hap-pening and getting it.

IT'S A CONFUSING FEELING. LIKE I'VE BEEN WRITING ABOUT POLICE ABUSES FOR A WHILE AND IT'S LIKE: "SEE? THIS IS WHAT I'VE BEEN SAYING." BUT OBVIOUSLY I WOULD PREFER THAT WE DIDN'T HAVE SO MANY EXAMPLES. IF YOU'RE OPTIMISTIC WHAT MIGHT YOU HOPE MIGHT COME OUT OF THIS MOMENT?

I think there's a decent chance the police secrecy law, Article 50-A will actually be overturned in New York state. It's one of the most powerful police secrecy laws in the country, and basically makes it impossible for us to get information about police misconduct. That makes it very hard to sue the police or to cross-examine them.

In my dream optimistic world we would defund the NYPD. The NYPD yesterday in their argument painted themselves as these poor victims who are just struggling, and said they're throwing Molotov cocktails at us, setting our police stations on fire, we're under attack, it's not fair, we're scared, we're doing the best we can. It's insane to me they could say that with a straight face considering there are 38,000 NYPD. They're one of the best-funded police departments in the world, if not the best. They have surveillance tools at their fingertips. It's unbelievable that they would say we can't handle it because we're this poor little baby police department.

THAT'S THE POLICE NARRATIVE. THEY'RE SUCH BABIES. THEY CAN'T JUST BRUTALIZE US, THEY ALSO HAVE TO BE THE VICTIMS THEMSELVES ALL THE TIME.

Yeah. I know it's what they always do so, again, I'm not surprised. But it's just so ridiculous to see them doing it. I really think they believe their own bullshit.

OBVIOUSLY LOTS OF PEOPLE KNEW THIS, YOU MENTIONED THE "GOOD LIBS" WHO STILL RESPECT THE POLICE, BUT I THINK SOME OF THEM ARE MAYBE STARTING TO REALIZE THAT THE POLICE LIE CONSTANTLY. ESPECIALLY WITH THAT STORY IN BUFFALO WITH POLICE ALMOST KILLING SEVENTY-FIVE-YEAR-OLD PEACEFUL PROTESTOR MARTIN GUGINO WHEN THEY PUSHED HIM OVER FOR NOTHING. IS THAT SOMETHING YOU'VE ENCOUNTERED IN YOUR CAREER?

Absolutely. I was actually thinking about it yesterday in court. They lie constantly. Especially in the press. The *New York Post* here is the cop conservative paper. It's lie after lie after lie. It happened with bail reform. They lied about people who got out on bail committing new crimes, but it would be someone who got out on bail four years ago and they didn't even really get arrested. But also just in the police reports, and in terms of planting evidence on our clients, saying our clients were seen doing illegal things so they have an excuse to search people. It's just habitual lying. I think they do it because they get away with it. There are no repercussions. I work at Legal Aid, and there are 2,000 lawyers in my office, and we are fighting against that all the time. But when it's such a big systemic issue—there are individual cases we win on—but actually stopping the cops from lying requires judges to hold them accountable, and for the DAs to prosecute them when they do it. That doesn't happen.

ANOTHER THING PEOPLE ARE TALKING ABOUT LATELY IS HOW IT'S BASICALLY IMPOSSIBLE TO CONSUME TV IN AMERICA THAT ISN'T ABOUT COPS. IN THOSE SHOWS YOU ARE DEPICTED AS THE BAD GUY USUALLY. YOU, PERSONALLY, ARE JAMMING UP THE COPS WHO ARE JUST TRYING TO CLEAN UP THE STREETS. THE WEENIE LAWYERS COME IN TALKING ABOUT "RIGHTS." CAN YOU WATCH THOSE TYPE OF SHOWS?

I don't watch those shows because they just seem like such a lie to me. I will say though, since I started working as a public defender in Manhattan, I will occasionally watch *Law & Order*. It makes the conditions that the DAs work in look really nice. These nice offices, all these resources. I've been to the DAs office many times in Manhattan and it's horrible. It's dirty and dingy and they share all these offices. I like to say, you know, I was watching *Law & Order* and it looked really nice there, is that what you expected you were gonna get? They say "shut up!"

But you're constantly bombarded with that in this country. The cops are the good guys. Law enforcement against the criminals and the lawyers that help them.

One other thing that's been really great for me and my colleagues, under Trump really, people have started to realize that public defenders actually do good stuff. It's been nice to hear people say "hey, good work guys." We don't do it for respect or else we'd get a different job, but it's a nice change.

WHAT'S THE NEXT STEP FOR YOUR CASE ON THESE DETENTIONS?

We're going to file a notice of appeal. Like I said since we filed the writ the number of people officially being held are way down. We think that we freaked them out and they started getting their shit together. What we do next depends on how they fix it. All those other things I mentioned, moving people around, or holding people that shouldn't be held period are the big next steps. We think that there are protestors that are just sitting somewhere, and because they weren't officially arrested they don't have to tell us about it. We don't know where those people are. We know that they are not being given access to lawyers and allowed to make phone calls. Since they're not officially arrested, all the rules about once you're arrested you have rights, they're saying those don't apply. That's a huge violation of people's rights.

SEEMS LIKE THE PEOPLE ALWAYS MOANING ABOUT THE CONSTITUTION WOULD BE UPSET ABOUT THIS. THAT'S LITERALLY ONE OF THE MOST IMPORTANT PRINCIPLES, YOU CAN'T BE SECRETLY DETAINED BY THE POLICE.

Yes. I think there will be several more writs of habeas corpus and lawsuits. We're trying to decide what to do next. I'm just doing a small part of this. My unit does police accountability stuff so we've got twenty different fires we're trying to put out all the time.

Like I said, this is all stuff we knew about already. I think we're more ready than most people to respond to it. Whether the judges actually do what's right is another question. But we'll keep trying.

A week later I spoke with Goodman again and their appeal had managed to get hundreds released and things moving more speedily in the courts. It wasn't all good news though.

"In the last week we've seen some major changes," she told me. "They repealed 50-A [the law shielding police disciplinary records], arraignments are moving quickly, and a federal judge kicked ICE out of the courts."

"But this has also been a week of devastation as more and more stories come out about the NYPD's handling of the protests," she said.

"The stories of gleeful abuse and brutality are absolutely heartbreaking. They continue to beat, pepper spray and illegally detain peaceful protesters. We are working to stop them on several fronts, including lawsuits, more writs of habeas corpus, and changes to the law. The changes we've seen in the last week wouldn't have been possible without such a powerful, people-led movement, and there is real fear that the movement will lose steam and be co-opted by the mainstream. I hope that everyone is starting to understand just how rotten the police truly are and will look to the people behind this movement for guidance on how to effect true and lasting change."

As regards their original habeas corpus case it's still going ahead even though the issue of detaining people for over twenty-four hours pre-arraignment has abated.

"We are moving forward on the appeal because we want to challenge the precedent and make it impossible for future judges to make similarly outrageous decisions," she said. "We are also challenging the illegal detention of peaceful protesters. The police have been illegally detaining people in large numbers and 'disappearing them' for hours or days at a time. These protesters, who are not part of the writ of habeas corpus because they are not charged with 'arrestable offenses,' are beaten and gassed and then rounded up and refused access to their attorneys and medical care, tortured with zip ties to the point of their hands bleeding, subjected to extreme heat, and held in dangerous conditions. We continue to fight for the release of people that have already been detained and find ways to stop the police from doing this as the protests continue."

I'VE BEEN SLEEPING WITH A SHOVEL UNDER THE BED

I've been sleeping with a shovel under the bed. It wasn't my first choice. I rifled through the shed out back selecting potential weapons one by one like a montage in a shitty zombie movie: the metal rake the rusty garden shears the Weedwacker. The lawnmower seemed impractical. An important consideration when deciding which weapon to go to sleep with isn't just what you could use it for on the off chance you have to but also how much damage you could do to yourself when you inevitably stub your fucking toe on it in the middle of the night after you wake up to piss from a dream about how your high school football coach is disappointed in you or whatever it is men dream about. Indignities you've suffered. Glories that fell just out of your grasp but if only you had the chance to do them over again. Assorted pervert shit.

It's been a couple weeks now and mercifully I haven't had to swing the shovel at any intruder's head but for a while there I wasn't so sure. It was a warm evening and I'd just gotten back from a sweaty humid march in Cambridge through streets that are so familiar to me but that seem transformed now in the way a place you used to go every day changes on you the second you turn your back. I came home angry and emotional but invigorated as one does from any march to my new neighborhood that still doesn't seem familiar to me and heard someone outside blasting Rush Limbaugh on the radio and yelling to themselves. ALL LIVES MATTER! he said. ALL LIVES MATTER! Just gassing himself up about the thugs and looters and what have you. You know the script. My own private live performance of a nightly Tucker Carlson monologue.

I mentioned earlier that when we first moved in we hooked up the WiFi and saw a nearby network was TRUMP2020 and we were immediately demoralized. Goddamnit who's this fucking guy I thought. Kind of wish I never found out.

Naturally being me I went outside to tell the yelling guy to go fuck himself and eat shit and fuck off and things of that nature. It devolved pretty quickly from there as you can imagine. It wasn't exactly my most trenchant oratory performance. He said he was a veteran and I called him a baby killer and he said any of them that he did kill had it coming. Picture two tired idiot dogs barking at each other from the perimeter of their leashes. THIS TYPE OF SHIT IS NOT WELCOME HERE I yelled.

Thankfully it ended after a while when other people came out to inspect what the fuck was happening. This area isn't exactly a hotbed of street fights as best I can tell so far. I woke up embarrassed that all my new neighbors had heard me talking like that.

The next afternoon the solo porch ranting continued from his end but strangely it was me that felt bad about my role in the whole thing. I had been so fucking cruel to this stranger it was weighing on me. To be sure I did nothing wrong per se I simply told a racist to shut the fuck up but I didn't like who I was when I was doing it. I was some much uglier person. Righteous and correct but still ugly. Even if someone has it coming you might not like how it feels to deliver it to them.

The day after that the police arrived. We did not call them to be clear it was another neighbor who felt threatened. Apparently they had seen the guy waving a machete around and spouting off in our direction. Four police cars pulled up outside his house and he ran inside yelling back at them from out the window. He has rifles inside he said.

Jesus Christ I thought am I going to have to side with the guy who wants to kill me against the cops now just out of political principle? Leave that guy alone you fucking cops!

The police left after about a half hour because I guess it's not technically illegal to wave a machete around in your own yard even if you're doing it in such and such a way. It's not technically illegal to yell to the police you have guns inside although tbh that particular detail seemed to merit further investigation in my opinion but what can you do. It's not technically illegal to film your neighbor's house and say these people called the cops on me over and over either.

I am pretty certain I had told him how much I do not like the cops the night before and I tried to explain to him from across the way that it wasn't me who called them but apparently he wasn't in the mood to talk. It was pretty hilarious to me that I had to hurriedly try to explain to a guy I was in a potentially violent conflict with not to worry I am not the type of guy to call the police. I'm cool man. Fuck you though but I'm cool.

Isn't this kind of fascinating I said to Michelle. Here we are presented with our very own conundrum about what to do when it comes to calling the police for help or not. Again I didn't call them but when they appeared they basically poked around the block for a while then said eh nothing to be done here and peaced out. Michelle did not find it a particularly intriguing ethical quandary at the time. Or at least that wasn't the most salient issue at hand what with all the worrying about being killed in the air.

That night I got the shovel and we went off to restless sleep. The next few days and nights we did the same peeking out the window hoping we wouldn't hear the telltale harbinger of conflict that the sound of a right-wing radio talk show came to symbolize.

A day or so later when I saw him outside I went out to try to talk but he avoided me. This is no way to live I thought. It felt like what it feels like to live in a physically abusive home like there was a heavy weighted blanket draped over everything. Maybe if we make ourselves small and silent he won't notice us and we'll stay safe this time.

We had been managing fine enough during the pandemic but constantly stressed like the rest of you are too. We had been gnashing our teeth at the news every night at the dozens and dozens of images of police brutality but through it all we at least had a home to feel safe in until we didn't.

More than anything I wanted some sort of resource for conflict de-escalation. I didn't want the police to break down his door and engage in a shoot-out. I didn't want the guy to go to jail or get in any kind of trouble. I just wanted someone to be able to mediate a discussion. Not that I imagined we would become friendly or find common ground despite our differences or anything dumb like that but more to turn down the heat somewhat so that we could all go about our business without looking over our shoulders. Someone said to call the local court and ask if they have some sort of victims services thing and I did and they had me call some other District Attorney guy or whatever and he had me call someone else and the long and short of all that was ah that's too bad ummm don't know what to tell you see ya.

I am not afraid of fighting a guy. I don't want to especially when I'm thinking clearly but I'll do it if I have to. It's likely in very many of those hypothetical scenarios I would get my ass kicked but that is just how it is. I am on the other hand definitely not interested in being shot to death or having my dick hacked off with a machete. Men spend a lot of time envisioning themselves as John Wick dispatching assailants easily but I'm not stupid enough to think there's anything I could do in a situation like that besides die and then as I'm dying think ah I fucked up on this one.

The absurdity of this all happening as tens of thousands of people marched and clashed in the streets was palpable for me. I had felt badly some days not always being out there and being more or less safely tucked away in the suburbs now. I felt badly about not getting my head stomped in by the cops and for not placing my body in the grinder often enough. Maybe this was my way of doing penance for that by bringing conflict to my neighborhood? But after a protest or riot you can at least if you aren't arrested usually go home and sleep soundly in your own bed. Don't shit where you eat I guess.

Throughout it all I still felt badly about being mean to this fucking guy though. What is that? Is that empathy? Perhaps there's some PTSD type of situation going on over there and if so we did that to that guy. Not us specifically but all of us. We train these dudes to go kill for nothing and then when they come back we say fuck you good luck out there.

What a weird internal conflict to have. To feel like you bullied a MAGA guy too harshly. Does that make me a pussy or just a human being?

On top of it all I felt terrible about potentially putting Michelle in danger with my big fucking mouth.

Ok so here's the real humiliating part. After feeling like I was living inside of a delayed sneeze for a week or more I decided I had to put it all to an end one way or another. I noticed the neighbor seemed to enjoy gardening with or without a machete so I drove down to this sad little dusty flower shop around the corner with about five plants total in stock and asked the lady what one in particular was. This plant uh doesn't have any kind of menacing symbolism to it or anything does it I asked. It's not the I'm going to kill you plant by any chance is it and she said no it was a peace lily and I thought that's a little on the nose but I bought it anyway and brought it home. I wrote a note saying I was sorry for starting a fight and let's just try to live quietly and peacefully. I tried to put myself in his shoes. After all I was the one that came storming over to his property trying to start shit. There's nothing in the rules that says you can't talk back to racist radio shows on your own porch right? That's the American dream baby! Maybe I was the bad guy?

How fucking shameful though lol. I bought my MAGA neighbor a housewarming gift and basically said sorry I was mad that you were very loudly racist.

I left the plant on the porch and we watched through the blinds as he brought it inside and considered it then promptly put it back out on the street. Shit shit shit.

But then later on that night it was gone. Did they think better of it and take it back in? Did they throw it out? No way to know at this point. But things have been quiet for about ten days now and it feels a lot better than how it felt before. Now we just live in a country with a rapidly accelerating pandemic and constant police violence everywhere to worry about. It feels like the good old days of a month ago again. There's always a more uncomfortable and menacing level of Hell World to dig down into that makes the last one seem like a vacation.

I'm not sure what the lesson is here or if there's a lesson at all. There usually aren't lessons or at least not discernible tidy ones. Apologize to more racists?

I asked Michelle what she thought the lesson was just now and she said something about how people who always ask what are you going to do if you need to call the cops someday should know that they're probably just gonna come poke around and play with their balls for a bit then leave having solved nothing. Not in those exact words but like that. And then she said maybe the lesson for me personally is to learn not to escalate things with anger despite how I might feel about confronting white supremacy or being an ally or something like that but that part was about me changing so I didn't really pay attention.

Or maybe the whole stupid affair just reminds us of the most American lesson of them all which is if you get enough guns you never have to say you're sorry. If you're capable of enough potential violence much like the police themselves then you get to be the scary one and the victim at the same time. It's the perfect system.

THIS COMMUNAL GRIEF SPILLS OVER AND IT'S ALMOST BEAUTIFUL

On Friday May 29 journalist Linda Tirado was covering the uprising in Minneapolis when she was shot in the eye by law enforcement despite clearly identifying herself as press. She was rushed to surgery soon after but doctors were unable to save her vision. I spoke with Tirado—the author of *Hand to Mouth: Living in Bootstrap America*—about what happened that night, the lawsuit she's bringing against the police, and where she goes from here.

WHAT WERE THE CIRCUMSTANCES OF YOU BEING SHOT?

I had gotten into Minneapolis on Thursday evening and did some work on location. That was the first night the National Guard was there. Friday was the first night of curfew, which press were meant to be exempted from. I was maybe a block or two from the 3rd precinct at a Wells Fargo watching a car burning at the drive-through. We saw protesters coming from the direction of the precinct and they said they had been gassed. I asked if they heard any warning and they said no.

I put on my mask and respirator and I went to take photos. I was lining up my establishing shot when I got hit in the face.

WITH A RUBBER BULLET?

We believe it was a 40mm compressed foam bullet. The Minneapolis PD is very staunchly on record with *The New York Times* saying they haven't used rubber bullets in twenty years. So depending on what we're calling our rounds that blind people these days. . .

THIS IS KIND OF A STUPID QUESTION, BUT WHAT WAS YOUR REACTION? DID YOU KNOW SOMETHING REALLY BAD HAD HAPPENED RIGHT AWAY?

Yeah, my first reaction was, oh fuck, this isn't good. My goggles came off. I was wearing protective eye gear. Any photographer working in tear gas is gonna need that. I had a laceration on my eyebrow that was bleeding freely, and the gas started hitting me. So I squeezed my eyes shut and started screaming that I'm press. I remember somebody came and took my arm and said we're going to take you to the medics. Then we ran for a little while. I don't know how long. Somebody patched up my eye, and they tossed me in a janky old van and drove me to the hospital.

WAS THERE ANY HOPE OF TRYING TO SAVE YOUR EYE OR WAS IT TOO LATE?

It was pretty far gone. I remember I tweeted from the hospital that I was going into surgery and they were going to try to save the eye. I didn't really have a good conception if that meant the vision or the organ. I woke up the next day and they were like, well, the good news is you don't have Covid, we had to test you before surgery. The bad news is you're blind. I was like, alright, cool. I remember thinking all you have to do to get basic medical care is get shot in the face.

DO YOU HAVE INSURANCE?
No!

ARE YOU FUCKED?
Oh completely. I'm in for $58,000 so far between two surgeries. And those are just the ones I know about. I've got a few more surgeries coming up, so ... The hospital called me yesterday for the first time since emergency surgery, and it was some lady who wanted to sign me up for Minnesota Medicaid. I'm not a resident so she said call these other people. I called them and they said we can't help you you're not a resident, call these other people. All of them had a different number that I owed them. I finally got through to the business office and they said we can set you up on a payment plan. We gave you an uninsured discount, so you only owe us $29,000. You can pay us $2,900 a month for the next ten months and you're good to go.

VERY SIMPLY!
I laughed so hard the lady started laughing. I explained to her there's no fuck off way that's going to happen. So they've got me on $100 a month. It will take me just under twenty five years to pay off the first surgery.

IT'S LIKE PAYING OFF A FUCKING MORTGAGE ON LOSING YOUR EYE. THIS IS A TOTAL CONFLUENCE OF EVERYTHING THAT'S WRONG RIGHT NOW: POLICE VIOLENCE, THE HEALTHCARE INDUSTRY, THE PRESS BEING UNDER ATTACK. HAVE YOU THOUGHT ABOUT IT LIKE THAT, THIS SORT OF CONVERGENCE OF HISTORY HAPPENING ON YOUR BODY?
As a writer, and a memoirist particularly, yes, and it's fucking overwhelming. I haven't been able to wrap my brain around

all of that happening at once or how useful it could be made. The one thing I don't want to have happen is this happens and then nothing happens. Then what was the fucking point? I've been turning it over in my mind, what do we do with this. If I'm a character in my own story now, what's the arc there? What does the story need for it to be worthwhile somehow?

I'M SURPRISED FROM WHEN WE TALKED YESTERDAY, AND SOME OF YOUR TWEETS—I THINK YOU JOKED RIGHT AWAY ABOUT AT LEAST IT WASN'T YOUR CAMERA EYE—YOU SEEM TO BE IN SURPRISINGLY DECENT SPIRITS.
I worked minimum wage for twenty years. It's really hard for something shitty to happen and for me not to joke about it. I worked in too many bars. I deployed my husband, a marine, to Fallujah. It's not been the easiest life. I think the thing you learn when you work in service for near two decades is how to make other people comfortable with how much shit they're putting on you.

YOU WROTE A BOOK ABOUT THAT.
It's called *Hand to Mouth: Living in Bootstrap America*. It's basically 288 pages of It sucks to be poor. It surprised me that it was really well received, because for years now I've heard all these upper-middle-class people saying they never really thought about it. I literally had a paragraph where I said $7.25 x 40 x 52 = fuck you. I did the math, and people were like, I've never stopped to do that before. I'm talking about masters of the fucking economy over here. How did you not know? How did you never stop to think about what it's like for millions of people when you run this bitch?

I think the only reason I'm dealing with this so well is I think poverty and low-wage work is just as brutal and visceral as losing an eye to a police bullet. It's just that people don't think of it that way because it happens to more people.

I WRITE A LOT ABOUT HOW WE'RE SUBJECTING PEOPLE TO VIOLENCE CONSTANTLY. NOT JUST THE OVERT TYPE OF VIOLENCE LIKE SHOOTINGS, BUT TRYING TO SURVIVE IN A HOSTILE FUCKING COUNTRY. IT'S A WARZONE FOR SO MANY PEOPLE JUST TRYING TO LIVE.

I think that's true. When you work manual labor, and I've worked on pig farms, and on factory floors, all of the shit jobs that nobody wants to do because they maybe at least pay $10 an hour. When that's your job you kind of know that you're going to be permanently disabled at some point, and it's a crapshoot for how many good years you're going to get. I think that's helping me deal with this too. I'm thirty-seven. I got thirty-seven good years. I've got friends who came back from the war. I graduated high school in 1999 and a lot of dudes I knew enlisted and came back real fucked. I know a ton of kids that lost shit in farming accidents or factory accidents. I know a kid who put his hand in the deep fryer at a Wendy's. I made it to thirty-seven man. I did ok. And how fucking bleak is that?

WHERE DID YOU GROW UP?

Utah. I live outside Nashville now. I moved around a lot in the last five years since the book happened. I went to Australia for some time. I spent a lot of time in the UK. I embedded in Ferguson. I embedded in Malheur when the Bundys took over for three weeks. Finally my kids are old enough they were like, "Mom, we can't move anymore. We need friends." So we settled. And that turned out to be a good decision because soon after we settled I got shot in the fucking face!

SO YOU'RE SUING NOW?

We're suing the departments that were there and the people in charge of those departments. We're not 100 percent sure which agencies would have fired. We know based on the orientation of my body and the shot that I was lining up that it came from the police line. And we have no reports of protesters using projectiles that could cause this type of injury. They were throwing bottles. It wouldn't have been a ballistic projectile like this. So we're suing for damages, and further, for injunctive relief. It's unfortunate that we have to have the courts declare that you can't shoot a working member of the press in the face. But it seems like that might be an important declaration to underscore at this point.

HAVE ANY OF THE THINGS YOU ALREADY KNEW ABOUT HOW BAD THINGS HAVE ALWAYS BEEN BEEN REINFORCED FOR YOU THE PAST COUPLE WEEKS?

No, I think the thing that's come over me in the last couple weeks is holy shit I didn't know we were already this far down the path already. I was in Ferguson for six weeks initially, and have been back over the years. I thought St. Louis cops were going to be the worst I ever saw. Then I got to Minneapolis and I was like, holy fuck, it's next level up here. Which is something you have heard. People had told me you're going to Minneapolis, be careful, those guys don't fuck around. But to this level, of blinding multiple people. I keep going back and forth. I'm not sure whether it would be more morally upsetting if they targeted and intentionally shot people, or whether they were just firing indiscriminately at head level into a crowd. That's the thing that keeps trapping my mind. Which would I be more angry at? Neither of those are acceptable strategies.

RIGHT. ONE IS PURPOSEFULLY MALEVOLENT AND ONE IS INDIFFERENTLY . . .

Homicidal. If I hadn't been wearing my goggles, the fact that it was a soft part of my face . . . god knows . . .

IT COULD'VE BEEN MUCH WORSE. HAS IT HARDENED YOUR RESOLVE TO GET BACK TO WORK?

I was back at work five hours after they let me out of the damn surgery. I was in my hospital bed running down leads. I don't know if I'm ever going to be able to cover as a frontline observer anymore. Largely because you don't want to be a danger to everyone around you. They say monocular vision is very specific and kind of a little whimsical even with what you'll be able to see, your depth perception and things like that. So it's a question of waiting to see if I'm going to be a hazard to other people. Will I be tripping over curbs if I have to run. So we don't know if I'll be able to get back to that particular beat, but it's not going to stop me from reporting out these stories. It might just mean I can't take my own photos.

THE BIG THING PEOPLE ARE TALKING ABOUT IN THE MEDIA THIS PAST WEEK, THE "FREE SPEECH" SHIT HEADS, IS "CANCEL CULTURE." DOESN'T IT SEEM ABSURD THAT THAT SORT OF THING IS AN OBSESSION FOR A LOT OF PEOPLE WHEN THE POLICE ARE OUT HERE ACTIVELY BRUTALIZING PEOPLE OVER THEIR FIRST AMENDMENT RIGHTS? IT'S INSULTING.

I think it's absurd on the face of it, but in another way it makes absolute perfect sense. You've got a whole lot of people that are invested in not knowing that this is what it's like. And a whole lot of people who would have to take a good hard look at themselves and what they're willing to sacrifice. It turns out it's nothing. They wouldn't give up . . . 5 percent of their salary to bend things toward justice.

They live in their places and they want to keep them and in order to they have to go along with this fantasy of "a few bad apples." I've seen this going around Twitter: You do realize the entire point of that whole metaphor is that it spoils the entire bunch? That's how the oxygenation works you asshole.

YOU MENTIONED YOU'VE BEEN GETTING A LOT OF ATTENTION ONLINE NOW, BOTH GOOD AND BAD. ARE PEOPLE GIVING YOU A REALLY HARD TIME?

It seems to be two-pronged on the negative stuff. Any woman writer, or any woman of any public note, is going to have her DMs full of dudes that are like, hi, hi, hi, hey sexy. Now it seems to have turned over into, "You shouldn't have been there. It's your own fault you got shot in the face." Just all these dudes like why did you put yourself in front of soldiers? Well it's my fucking job dude. Do you not like the idea of knowing what your country is doing?

Then there's a ton of people who are super well-meaning and lovely, and they all have advice on what I should do. It's been really interesting, because a good portion of my public work since I got hit has been saying don't infantilize me. I'm a writer. I can find my own words for this. You don't have to tell me how to define this. You don't have to tell me what my legal strategy should be. I got one of the best law firms in the country. I'm perfectly capable. If I could hold my own as a low-wage worker speaking up to Stanley McChrystal I think I can manage this.

PEOPLE LOVE TO TELL PEOPLE WHAT TO DO! ARE YOU HEARTENED BY WHAT WE'RE SEEING? DO YOU THINK THIS IS A SERIOUS MOMENT OF CHANGE?

I think it's a shift for some people. I've been using the fascism word openly since 2015. I've been writing about it, because I was raised by right-wing western conservatives, people who worship Rush Limbaugh. So when Trump came up it spiked this nativist part of my brain and I thought oh, this is going to be bad. I think what's happening is we're finally seeing a lot of people understanding how bad it is. They couldn't see it coming, they had to wait until it was enacted on their friends' bodies. The fact that so many of these protests are white, which you didn't see for Ferguson, which was supposed to be a change- everything flashpoint, and you didn't see this kind of response. I don't know that it changes anything but I think that it changes the game board. I don't know that it changes the outcome yet, I don't think we've hit that level, but I think the landscape has changed. That is going to be interesting to see. You know, that kid up in Fort Wayne lost his eye. I'm two years younger than his mom. He's just out of school. Those things radicalize you when it's your son or daughter. The suburban moms who are out there like "Fuck you Donald Trump." You wouldn't have seen that three months ago.

WHAT ARE YOU WORKING ON NOW?

I'm not putting too much pressure on myself to create, which is hard for a freelancer. I don't have very much time I can keep my eyes open at a stretch right now, as my right eye gets used to taking the whole weight. I sat down yesterday and said I'm going to play this bullshit video game from 1999, but in the back of my head I was like I should really be pitching right now. I had a whole argument with myself. You just got shot in the face you're allowed to not pitch for an hour.

I THINK YOU CAN TAKE A FEW DAYS OFF.

Yeah but you know, your brain just won't let you.

WELL DID YOU AT LEAST GET ANY GOOD PHOTOS OUT OF THE DEAL?

Dude I got some amazing shots. I was there for the days Minneapolis was burning. It's an unfortunate part of our work that the worse shit is the better the photos are. I got some incredible pictures of rainbows and structure fires and rainbows and tear gas. People with clenched fists outlined against the chaos. And the joy of it. I picked up some of the joy in these photos. That's the part you can never explain to anybody. They think it's all pillaging and burning and looting. But it's the first time that this rage . . . this communal grief. It spills over and it's almost beautiful.

I DIDN'T REALIZE MY BLOOD AND BONES WERE NEXT

It's the middle of June and as more states have begun the process of ~~opening back up~~ I was curious how it's going for the service workers who have to risk their lives so we can pretend everything is normal again. A dozen or so of them from around the country—waiters, salon and retail workers, librarians, and others — told me how they feel and how customers have been treating them.

- Nobody is concerned with sanitation procedures at the restaurant in Milwaukee I work at. If anything, they find them annoying. We have a touchless payment system where customers can pay on their phones and a few of my tables seemed bothered by it. Also no one is using hand sanitizer other than the staff.

- Most people are very considerate in the neighborhood coffee shop I work at in Pittsburgh. No one seems to care about social distancing in practice though. Also people reflexively lean around the sneeze guard-style shields so they're basically useless. We reopened a week and change ago, although we'd been doing contactless pickup through quar. It's been mostly slow, which is good, but when it gets busy it can be really overwhelming in ways it never was before. Most people are good to us and understand where we're at, but there's still a few clowns every day who wanna try to educate us about how this is all made up and the masks don't matter or whatever.

· I went in for a shift on Thursday which was a very rainy day and we still had people come in to sit on the patio for reservations at my restaurant in Boston. The guests weren't taking to the guidelines seriously, like they couldn't wait to get their masks off. There were a few people who didn't have masks at all. I live with someone who is immunocompromised and I kind of freaked out to my general manager and he tried to talk me down and was basically saying the pandemic is over and that I would be fine. I completely freaked out at him at this point because he's basically saying it's worth it if a family member of mine dies so that a couple Karens can drink wine on our rainy patio.

I left and they said they'll call me in a few weeks. I know not everyone can afford to tell their boss to fuck off right now and honestly I'm not sure if I can either. I'm also not sure if I'll ever go back.

It feels like a disaster movie in real time. I couldn't believe what my manager was saying. I was like there are 1,800 new cases in Florida today and he acted like that's a Florida problem not a Massachusetts problem.

I made a joke to someone before the shift about how the machine of capitalism runs on blood and bones and, like, I didn't realize my blood and bones were next.

· I work at a salon in Oklahoma City. People are pissed they have to wear masks and they are tipping less than normal. I'm going to get sick and not be able to afford it because Karen wants her butthole waxed.

It's the middle of Trump country. They think it's a conspiracy theory and they're worried about us wearing masks because they think we're going to get CO_2 poisoning, and then they tip us a dollar after their Brazilian.

I'm actually making about 20 percent less than I usually do on my checks. But we're in Phase 3 reopening in our state, even though people are dying all around us. The governor is a fucking idiot who doesn't vote and has no political experience.

I had a client who complained about the mask requirement and the Covid precautions we are required to take. She was worried BLM protesters were going to come in and rape her during her service at eleven in the morning. How does one respond to that level of hysteria?

· Today is my fourth day back at a neighborhood restaurant in Ohio and people who have been coming out mostly think everything about Covid was a hoax. Some are just bored and need somewhere to go. Overall it's a strange vibe. It feels like it's not gonna last for some reason.

I don't feel comfortable seeing any loved ones because of how chill the guests are about the risk. I've seen two masks in four days. All the employees are masked up though. We have to wear masks while guests are in the building, they aren't required to wear any, and we have 60 percent capacity. Other than the masks, I've had my temp checked once. It's the same job that it was before this all started. The guests are taking it super chill, to the point where they always ask us to take our masks off while we serve them—we don't—and freak out when we tell them we can't leave their water on the tables anymore etc. It's in a richer white area in my city. It just feels like because of how relaxed the customers are that it's not gonna last all summer. A little more than half of them are above forty-five too. Young people are coming in but it's plenty of older folks who should care a little more.

• I work at a coffee shop in Toronto. We reopened just over a month ago. At first people were doing really well about wearing masks, maintaining distance, and observing our one customer capacity, but every week people care less and less. It feels like people are treating it like a New Year's resolution diet. They were trying really hard for two weeks, slipped a little bit towards the end of the month, and will give up when they don't see immediate results.

- After three months of being a waste of a human due to this shit I went back to work. I'm the director of a few properties throughout Massachusetts. It's my first week back and there's already a Covid positive at one of them. I worked side by side with this person for two days, listening to him cough in his mask. I told the chef he needed to address the problem of workers getting sick. He didn't. We closed again and I'm in quarantine as a precaution. The industry is fucked. I'm feeling pretty negative right now, and trying real hard not to be. My biggest concern is our undocumented hourlies. We take temps and have them fill out all the paperwork, but there's zero chance they're gonna go home instead of making a paycheck. There's no unemployment available for them. I don't blame them but it's gonna put us all in jeopardy. These are some of my favorite humans and friends. We've done what we can to help them through this shit time. It's an unfortunate and frightening reality of what's to come.

- I work at a restaurant in Cleveland. It's been alright, but I've already noticed a decline in tips and people generally just back to their entitled antics. When I first started back we were doing takeout only, but we opened for dine-in a couple of weeks ago. Between this and the protests and everything happening people have not been as understanding or respectful as you'd hope, although expecting anything is a mistake to be sure. The state handed down no real safety procedures, so everything from masks to keeping everything six feet apart has come down to us.

We're required to wear masks and gloves but our owner doesn't want to ask the customers to do anything, so there's no requirements for the patrons at our place, just the workers unfortunately.

The thing that's definitely driving me the most insane so far is how many people come in and then are absolutely appalled other people have the nerve to be at our restaurant as well. People come in with no masks and crowd around my host stand and then I get freaked out and then they're mad because "they don't feel safe."

There's a lot of pressure being put on us low-wage employees to do our jobs and then make people "feel good about being out."

- The majority of people come into the restaurant in Colorado not wearing masks. No one seems to be worried about actual sanitary measures or social distancing. Mostly they want to tell you how stupid it all is, or ask how much wearing the mask all day sucks. There's been an increase in hissy fits over perceived mistakes. But for the most part customers are acting the same. Some express anger at the new measures, some like to try to take a stand about not wearing a mask. Mostly every table wants to talk about it and know what we're being told to do by corporate.

I am worried. I'm currently uninsured and a hospitalization would financially ruin me. Also I live with my brother, who has severe asthma, so while he is still working from home, I'm scared of infecting him. I would 100 percent not have gone back to work if I had the choice, but I was weary of unemployment fraud.

- I genuinely thought our regulars at the taproom — forty-five plus, white, semi-rural—would suck, but they've been super cool about respecting distance and bussing their own glassware. Tips have been solid. We're just outside of Portland . . . We're kind of a destination spot until Portland reopens. We don't require masks for customers, but all the employees wear them.

I was scared at first. I've kinda resigned myself to the fact that this is the new normal for the next year at least so whatever happens, happens. It fucking sucks ass but I'm stuck. I'm six months away from hitting my 20 percent vesting (ESOP) and if it wasn't for that I'd be long gone. At least I don't have to worry about being pulled over because of my skin color.

- I'm at a restaurant in Fairfield County, Connecticut. Just about every business here asks people to wear masks, as do we. So many people walk to the host stand with no mask. Once they get to the table there's no masks. I'm not six feet from them when I serve and take orders. I wear a mask except to take a break. People don't understand more than five people at a table creates congestion and less distance from other tables.

It makes me angry that people spent zero time reflecting on humankind and working on themselves to care more for others while they were locked down. We are a society that more or less only cares about ourselves and no one else.

POLICE HAVE NEVER ACTED IN SOLIDARITY WITH OTHER WORKERS

It's July and a group called Strike for Black Lives recently held a day of action. Among a number of other things in their hopes of establishing of a more equitable and just society they shared a reminder that "every worker has the opportunity to form a union, no matter where they work."

"Every worker in America must have the freedom that comes from economic security and equity in opportunity," they said. "We demand the immediate implementation of a $15/hour minimum wage, fully-funded healthcare coverage, and paid sick leave for all."

A second group who echoed their demands and encouraged a number of other further steps beyond those is called No Cop Unions, a coalition of rank-and-file union members from around the country.

"No Cop Unions supports the July 20th Strike for Black Lives," the group explained, "and calls on union leadership at the local, state, and national levels to give further meaning to the action by disaffiliating from police, corrections officers, and immigration enforcement agent unions."

I spoke with Kim Kelly of No Cop Unions to learn more about why cops should not be considered workers and a number of other issues including the terrifying situation in Portland and why the left should think about arming themselves.

WHAT EXACTLY IS NO COP UNIONS?

No Cop Unions is a collective of union members and labor activists from all over the country. There are over fifty of us. We're working together for two major goals: to get the AFL-CIO to disaffiliate from the International Union of Police Associations, and also to get affiliates who have law enforcement in their ranks that aren't getting as much attention to do so as well, like the CWA, AFSCME, AFGE . . . There are cops everywhere throughout labor movements. IUPA gets a lot of attention because that's the only one under the AFL-CIO umbrella that is specifically for law enforcement, but they're all over the place. The goal is to drop the cops. To eradicate law enforcement from the labor movement because they have no place there.

WHAT HAPPENED WITH THE AFL-CIO RECENTLY? THEY SAID THEY WOULDN'T DISAFFILIATE?

God, it's been frustrating. The reason it kind of jumped into the spotlight was because my union, the Writers Guild of America East, passed a resolution calling on the AFL-CIO to kick out IUPA. We were the first union under their umbrella to call for that, and there have been others since, which is dope. So we forced the issue. They had to address it. They were like, ok, we hear you, but: no. The current leadership of the AFL-CIO is very entrenched in Democratic Party politics. They're very much reform-minded. I don't think there's anything radical left in the upper echelons of that structure. I think also there is this culture of appeasement toward the more right wing-leaning aspects of the movement. IUPA endorsed Trump. There are union members who are conservative, pro-Trump, who are probably even worse. That's just the reality of being part of an organization with millions of members. I think there's a hesitancy on the leadership's part to offend or upset that faction. But the kind of people that would be upset by our kicking out the cops, I think their numbers are shrinking in the broader scheme of AFL-CIO members and the working class in general. I think this idea of the working class has been very politically convenient for a lot of politicians, that it's a bunch of conservative white guys in hard hats. Those guys exist, but they're not the only game in town anymore. The working class is Black and Brown and female and queer and trans. It's not just guys like my dad anymore. Thank god.

INSTINCTIVELY TO ME IT MAKES SENSE. BUT IF YOU WANTED TO EXPLAIN TO SOMEONE WHY POLICE AREN'T WORKERS AND WHY THEY DON'T BELONG IN THE LABOR MOVEMENT, WHAT WOULD YOU SAY?

Well, they're agents of the state . . . Police have never acted in solidarity with other workers. They've never been interested in protecting the rights of workers. They're there to protect the interests of property and capital and power. They have never been on our side. Going back over the centuries, police have never stood beside us on a picket line, they've been there beating us and cracking our skulls. Some of the biggest events in labor history, like the Haymarket riots, were started by cops murdering striking workers at the McCormick Reaper Works in Chicago. When it comes down to the definition of a worker, bosses are management, and a cop is a boss with a gun. There's nothing that they have in common with actual workers. I think because the police are a diverse workforce with people from various walks of life there's this sort of inclination that people like to say, well, they're workers, they're working class. They're just regular guys. Well, ok, if a regular guy ironworker murders someone, he's gonna lose his job. Can you say that about these "regular guy" cops? You can't, because that's how the system is set up. It may seem reductive to go to an us-and-them framework, but honestly they started it.

THERE IS SOME DISAGREEMENT ON THAT ISSUE EVEN ON THE LEFT THOUGH RIGHT?

Sure. It's interesting. No one can agree on anything anymore, whether or not we're on the same team. But when it comes to the cops, I'm sure it speaks to the political circles that I travel in, but it's very rare that I will see anybody defending the cops unless I travel into the realm of mainstream reporters, which is a whole other rancid kettle of fish. When it comes down to the idea of expelling the police being in any way negative, there is a valid argument against it on the labor side in that, since police are public sector workers, there is this notion that if we kick out the cops that would open up an avenue for right-wing politicians who are already incredibly anti-union to use it as a way to attack other public sector workers like teachers. So that's something we're considering, but when it comes down to it we've seen how teachers have been treated and how police have been treated and we know who's getting a better deal.

And this is just speaking for me. I don't have all the answers. But I don't think that theory holds that much water. We're already at a point where public sector workers are getting fucked, and police are already going to be mollycoddled and protected no matter what they do.

A LOT OF THE STORIES WE SEE, ESPECIALLY ON SOCIAL MEDIA, WITH POLICE SAYING THE MOST INSANE SHIT, THAT'S PRETTY MUCH ALWAYS THE UNION HEAD. THE NYPD GUY, AND IN BOSTON THEY HAVE THIS POLICE UNION MAGAZINE THAT'S WRITTEN SOME OF THE MOST INSANE RACIST ARTICLES AND SHIT. IT FEELS LIKE POLICE UNIONS ARE WHERE A LOT OF THE WORST STUFF FROM POLICE IS COMING FROM.

Right because they're the mouthpieces. You only really hear about police unions when they've fucked up, and when they're in the press they're always on the defensive because one of their guys has done something unconscionable. Here in Philly, good lord, the police union here, there was this cop called, literally Joseph Bologna . . .

HE WAS THE GUY BEATING EVERYONE UP . . .

Yeah, and he actually faced some consequences, which is unheard of, and the police union had a rally for him. They made a T-shirt for him. It was this overwhelming display of support for one of their guys who beat up a bunch of college kids. The police union chief is always out there in the press saying shit, and it's like, you guys aren't even trying to not seem like villains here. The president of IUPA sent a letter to the head of the AFL-CIO after all this discussion about kicking them out, and it was a bunch of insane shit about how he was profiling police, saying it's disgusting that anyone would say there's racism in this country. The knee jerk reactions really don't do them any favors. I don't know who they're hiring to do their PR because that person is not holding up their part of the deal.

A LOT OF THE THINGS WE GET OUTRAGED ABOUT, WHEN THEY KILL SOMEONE OR BEAT THE SHIT OUT OF SOMEONE, IT'S THE UNIONS PROTECTING THEM FROM ACCOUNTABILITY. LIKE THE GUY WHO MURDERED GEORGE FLOYD MIGHT BE ABLE TO KEEP HIS PENSION I HEARD. AS FAR AS I KNOW ALL POLICE UNIONS DO IS PROTECT THE VIOLENT ONES FROM CONSEQUENCES.

Pretty much. I mean in every union contract the goal is to protect the workers, or in this case the cops, so it's not weird that they're trying to protect them. But the nature of their work and their behavior is such that they're being protected from committing these egregious crimes against humanity. That's not what a union contract should be for . . . The scale is completely different for them and any other kind of working person. And the way police unions use the deep-rooted political power . . . they can get away with a lot. Their contracts are a big part of why killer cops end up back on the street, and why the public doesn't get information about what happened. There's a phenomenon called the Law Enforcement Officers' Bill of Rights, which is a big part of the issue. Those get slapped into union contracts in a bunch of cities, and it gives police officers this whole bevy of other rights that no other worker is going to get that are specifically engineered to prevent them from facing consequences. That's how we end up with the Derek Chauvins of the world getting their huge pensions, or killer cops back on the street. We've seen the NYPD appeal the dismissal of the guy who killed Eric Garner. Unions shouldn't be used as weapons against the working class or people in general. They're perverting the entire idea of what a union should be and what collective organizing should be. It's just disgusting at this point.

I WAS GOING TO SAY IT'S LIKE TURNING THE IDEA OF WHAT A UNION IS SUPPOSED TO BE FOR ON ITS HEAD. IN THEORY YOU'RE SUPPOSED TO PROTECT WORKERS FROM POWER, AND POLICE UNIONS DO THE EXACT OPPOSITE. THEY INCREASE THE LEVEL OF HARM THE AVERAGE PERSON CAN FACE.

Right. One of the most hallowed tenants of the labor movement is that an injury to one is an injury to all. How the fuck do police unions fall into that? In the most basic terms it doesn't make sense that they've been able to have unions in the first place. And there are other options for them. They could have their own associations, but having access to the rights of collective bargaining gives them so much power that they don't need.

I think it was in Boston in like 1919, there were riots from police officers who tried to form a union, and the AFL-CIO was like, nah, it's too dangerous to give these state agents extra privileges. We can't trust them. Yeah, we can't trust them, so why do we still have them around? You used to get it, now . . . I don't know what kind of like Democratic pablum has rotted everyone's brains at the top, but we don't need them. They don't care about us. They see us as targets not comrades.

SO WHAT DO YOU WANT PEOPLE IN UNIONS TO DO? WHAT ARE THE PRACTICAL STEPS YOU'RE ASKING PEOPLE?

There are small things and big things. Individual members, on a basic level, talk to your coworkers about this issue and try to get them to understand where you're coming from. Then take that to your elected union officials and reps. Try to push it as high as you can to get more people to pay attention to it. In terms of bigger ideas, we put out this press release this week in solidarity with the Strike for Black Lives, and we're taking the approach of yes, and . . . We respect what their demands are, they're great, but we have some other ideas. Some of the things we're looking for, kicking out the cop union is obviously the big one, and then supporting divesting and defunding cops and prisons. It's all interlinked. Defunding the police won't do anything if the prison system is left to pick up the slack. We're advocating for reinvesting those funds into what we're calling life-affirming institutions like healthcare and education and mental health. All of the reasons people generally find themselves in bad situations, a lot of the time it's not their fault. There are all of these horrible social, economic, and political reasons why people are placed in circumstances where crime and violence happens. Getting to the root of that and addressing those causes is going to actually help things. Giving the cops $70 billion more so they can buy more insane military toys isn't going to help. Investing in a community center or mental health services for unhoused people . . . there is so much the cities need that they are not getting because the cops get so much. Philly is running out of money, but the police budget is still astronomical.

WELL IF YOU DON'T GIVE THE POLICE STEALTH BOMBERS AND MISSILES THEN IT'S GOING TO BE CHAOS.

Yeah the terrorists will have won! So prioritizing redistributing economic power, specifically to Black, indigenous, and people of color, the ones who have been disproportionately harmed and also shut out of conversations around making this shit happen. Just try to make things more equitable and less murderous. That seems like the kind of thing where the labor movement would be like, oh, yeah. That's a dunk. But here we are.

YOU WOULD THINK SO! HAVE YOU BEEN PAYING ATTENTION TO WHAT'S GOING ON IN PORTLAND WITH THE BORDER PATROL OR WHATEVER?

I'm not a fan! I have a lot of friends in Portland living through this and it's just terrifying. Because I spend too much time online I'm very fluent in the vagaries of the cancel culture free speech whatever bullshit, and the biggest story in the country is not Bari Weiss getting a different job where she stays rich and dumb. It's the fact that there are right-wing death squads disappearing protestors in major U.S. cities. Not only the federal government's implicit approval, but they sent them there. We're just in the beginning as far as I'm concerned. This shit is going to be bad. I think people maybe don't have the bandwidth to handle it because there's so much shit happening. Even if you're a person who follows the news, there's so much shit, all of it bad, it's hard to focus on anything, which is why things like this are allowed to happen. So they've already sent the National Guard into mad cities in the country. Yeah they've pulled away for the most part, but what happens if like the mayor of Boston gets a hair up his ass? What happens if the NYPD decides, oh yeah, we want to invite our new friends over to play in our sandbox? Things are really bad.

AND OF COURSE EVERY CONSERVATIVE IS LIKE, IT'S GOOD WHEN THE FEDERAL GOVERNMENT COMES AND TAKES OVER A STATE AGAINST THE GOVERNOR'S WISHES. ALL THE RIGHT-WING PEOPLE ARE LIKE, NO, FUCK YOU, WE LOVE HAVING THE FEDS TAKE OVER STATES, THE VERY FAMOUS AND WELL-KNOWN CONSERVATIVE POSITION TO HAVE.

I thought that they were anti-tyranny? That was their whole bumper sticker ideology. But maybe specific kinds of tyranny are chill? This is what I'm learning in real time alongside everyone else. Defend your rights and community and your property . . . but not like that.

WHEN IT'S THE ANTIFA MENACE IT'S OK.

And the whole Boogaloo thing factors in. There are people who maybe don't have the same politics as us . . . I think there are humans who aren't necessarily leftists or revolutionaries who also see this shit happening and are like, that seems bad? Maybe I should get involved? And some of them have guns. Man, 2020 has been garbage, but 2021 is gonna knock our teeth out. We don't even know what's coming.

MY FIRST THOUGHT WAS WHERE ARE THE 2A GUYS? THIS IS WHAT YOU'VE BEEN WAITING FOR MAN. THE TROOPS ARE IN THE STREETS. ISN'T THIS YOUR LITERAL FANTASY? TO BE ABLE TO GO FIGHT THOSE GUYS?

Those guys are cowards. They're protecting statues and working on their bunkers. In Philly those guys are chilling in Marconi Plaza protecting a statue of Columbus that no one even threatened. And now the city has taken it down, which is a very funny side note. That's the inherent flaw with that whole prong of ideology. They don't mean it. They mean it when it comes to them and their property and their neighborhood. Like if Black Lives Matter comes to one of their neighborhoods, like we've seen in small towns around the country, that's a problem. But if it's some liberal bastion full of people they don't like essentially being invaded by the government they're like, well that doesn't concern me.

THEY'RE NEVER GOING TO COME FOR ME PERSONALLY SO NOT MY PROBLEM. I KNOW YOU ARE A SUPPORTER OF THE LEFT ARMING THEMSELVES. I'M OPEN TO HEARING ARGUMENTS FOR THAT, ALTHOUGH I'M REALLY, REALLY ANTI-GUN. LET'S SAY WE ARMED OURSELVES TO PUSH BACK AGAINST THE FEDS TAKING OVER CITIES. WOULDN'T WE JUST GET IMMEDIATELY SMOKED? WHAT IS THE POINT OF EVEN HAVING MY SHITTY LITTLE GUN WHEN THEY COME IN WITH THE TANK?

That's valid.

I KNOW IT'S A COMPLICATED TOPIC, BUT PLEASE EXPLAIN IT ALL SUCCINCTLY WITHIN TWO MINUTES.

Well I can give you my perspective at least. Nobody who isn't already too far gone to reason with is thinking about mounting any kind of standing army or militia or proactive offense against the state. That's just asking to be blown to smithereens. In a lot of this discussion around arming the left it's not an offensive posture, it's a defensive one. For example, if twenty of us showed up trying to scrap with the cops, that's twenty funerals. It's stupid. But if we're at a protest and twenty of us are there open-carrying, not causing any issues, just establishing a presence, the cops are going to act differently when they try to come toward the protestors we're trying to protect. I say that because I've seen it in multiple situations in multiple cities. In Charlottesville before the real bad things happened, there were a bunch of us in a park with a perimeter established by this group called Redneck Revolt, which has disbanded by now. There were hordes of roving Nazis everywhere, but none of them came into that park because there were people outside of it like, nah. They were a deterrent.

The cops don't respect anyone who isn't a cop. It's a dark thing to think about, but when you're there and you're armed you're placing yourself closer to their level. So they see you as more of a person. You're not as much of a target. And that gives them pause. Maybe it won't keep them from brutalizing everybody, but it will make them think twice about it. It will make them maybe think a minute about their strategy instead of cracking everyone's skulls. It's more of a buffer than a threat the way I see it. There's also the fact that a lot of these leftist gun organizations are white people. I think this is a way that people that have that privilege, who might not immediately be brutalized by the cops . . . When you can put yourself between Black and Brown people and the police, and they know they have to, if not respect you, but at least take a minute to kind of consider things, you're going to make yourself more helpful.

I don't have any grand delusions about any of this. I don't think if shots were fired anything good would happen. You never want that to happen. If you show up somewhere with a firearm that is an automatic escalation, and you need to respect that and understand what that means. You should never want violence to happen. Your whole purpose being there is to make sure violence doesn't happen. Maybe there are other people who see it differently, but I would not want to work with them. That's dangerous and stupid.

People who hate guns . . . I totally understand. Why wouldn't you hate guns in this country? Honestly being in Charlottesville shifted my perspective on it. It was like, ok, the only people protecting us that day were these other leftist people with firearms. The only time I felt safe was in that park. Obviously things went south, but it wasn't their fault.

As much as it sucks that there are millions and millions of guns everywhere, I think understanding that they can be used in a way that isn't necessarily bad would be good for the left to, if not embrace, but think about a little bit. The Black Panthers were right about a lot of things.

WHEN YOU PUT IT THAT WAY. WHETHER WE'RE ARMED OR NOT, IF THEY WANTED TO, THEY COULD STILL GET OUR ASSES, BUT THEY MIGHT THINK TWICE I GUESS.

A couple extra seconds might save a couple lives.

WELL I'M GONNA GO GET A GUN!

This stuff is really interesting to me because gun culture has
been this impenetrable force of right-wing chuds for so long.
The more I think about it I see nuance here that doesn't ever
get teased out because we have the insane NRA death cult
and the opposite, the ultra-liberals who think anyone who's
breathed on a gun is bad.

TOO MUCH OF THE DAMAGE HAS ALREADY BEEN DONE

I love restaurants and bars perhaps more so than I should but something about this rush to get back to a wholly unrecognizable version of them while also being wildly unsafe and exploitive puts the lie to the whole thing being about an experience and not just consumption for consumption's sake. Nothing we are supposed to love about this shit—the atmosphere and the camaraderie and bonhomie even the pleasure of fine service—is available at this time it's been 86'd so all that's left is the process of spending money because you miss spending money and having people fetch things for you. Enjoy the alfresco asphalt patio though I guess.

It's July now and the concepts of social distancing and wearing a mask to avoid catching or spreading a deadly disease still remain at this late hour a partisan issue. Why is that? The president and Fox News is how. That's all. Thanks for coming.

Neither Fox News nor Trump invented the selfish individualistic self-mythology of the average American but they have certainly weaponized it and turned the concept of any type of self-sacrifice into a sign of weakness. Look no further than the absolutely insane-making Board of County

Commissioners meeting in Palm Beach, Florida this month for evidence of how truly deep this mind rot has set in.

While considering a mandatory order to wear face-masks the commissioners heard from a series of concerned citizens. "They want to throw God's wonderful breathing system out the door," one woman complained.

"There's not enough to make this a pandemic," another woman added. "This is a planned-demic. This is totally political and you know it and I'm asking you to cease-and-desist from the political agendas that you're being 'propaganded' [?] to stand with and try to hold us hostage as American citizens."

"You literally cannot mandate someone to wear a mask knowing that that mask is killing people, it literally is killing people," a third said.

"And we the people are waking up and we know what citizens arrest is because citizens arrests are already happening, ok? And every single one of you that are obeying the devil's laws are going to be arrested and you, doctor, are going to be arrested for crimes against humanity."

On one day this month in Florida alone there were over 10,000 new cases of coronavirus reported. There were over 55,000 in the United States total that same single day.

For that you can thank the piss poor messaging from Trump himself as well as the governors in states who seek his favor and Fox News and their ideologically adjacent media outlets.

None of which is to say that blue states and their leaders are off the hook—our ten-foot-tall moron governor in

Massachusetts who is supposed to have done a "good job" getting things under control here is set to open gyms this week. Believe me there is nothing I want more in the world than to get back to the gym to load up *Define the Great Line* by Underoath on the iPad mini and stack four plates on the bar instantly snapping my spine in half rendering myself out of commission for six months but I'm simply not going to go to a gym right now.

Also I would imagine that many of the twentysome-things we've seen pictures of crowding patio bars in Boston and New York and the like consider themselves "as liberal as anyone, but . . ." so this isn't to say northeast libs good/ southern conservatives bad but nonetheless the fact remains that much of this needless death falls on the MAGA chuds who refused from the very beginning to take this pandemic seriously for . . . well I still don't understand why.

Multiple polls have borne out the feeling that many of us have had that wearing masks has become another front in our eternal pointless culture war of shit.

"In recent months, mask-wearing has become <u>a partisan issue</u>," Pew <u>found</u>.

"This partisan divide is also found in the behaviors of the general public: Democrats and those who lean Democratic are more likely than Republicans and Republican leaners to say they personally wore a mask all or most of the time in the past month (76% vs. 53%). Even after controlling for differences in the COVID-19 health impact in the communities where people live, Democrats are more likely to say they personally wear a mask all or most of the time."

"Conservative Republicans are among the least likely to say they have worn a mask all or most of the time in the past month–49% say they've done so, compared with 60% of moderate Republicans. Liberal Democrats are the most likely to say they have worn masks (83% say they've done so all or most of the time, vs. 71% of moderate Democrats)."

"Indeed, news media diet—or the top news sources people use—is strongly associated with coronavirus-related preventive practices," according to Gallop. "A partisan gap in attitudes and self-reported behaviors has existed since March and is growing larger. A significant contributor to this widening gap seems to be Americans' news media diet . . . lending support to the thesis that public health issues have become the newest extension of an ongoing culture war waged daily by partisan news outlets."

Although a number of national polls have shown a majority of partisans on either side regularly wearing a mask small state-by-state polls like this one in Iowa bear out the stubborn refusal to do so by the right.

"Iowa Democrats are more than twice as likely as Republicans to say they wear face masks or facial coverings almost all or most of the time when they're in public places indoors, a new Des Moines Register/Mediacom Iowa Poll shows," according to the *Des Moines Register.*

"Among Iowa Democrats, 76% say they do so, the poll shows. Among Iowa Republicans, 37% say they do. Among political independents, 52% say they do."

That could potentially be changing however! Maybe? Hopefully?

lol probably not we're fucked.

Yesterday George Abbot in Texas finally at long last issued an order for most counties in the state—which is currently getting its dick kicked off with new cases—to wear masks. He had long dragged his heels on the issue. I'm sure Texans by and large will be fine going along with it if I know anything about Texas which is the America of America.

That comes as Fox News is said to be pivoting to taking the pandemic seriously and encouraging mask use now but they already did this back and forth two-step a couple months ago and they're not to be trusted in any case nor afforded any measure of credit for belatedly doing the right thing. Too much of the damage has already been done.

Mercifully my own family who I may have mentioned I do not exactly see eye to eye with seem to have been taking things seriously all along. My mother an avid sewer and knitter made lovely masks and mailed them out to us and others a while back and my sisters (one of whom recovered from a mild case) seem to be going crazy with their children at home for so long but they are keeping to themselves as best I can tell. My dad who has fucking leukemia has gone back to work but he's in a room by himself and wearing a mask while there so . . . It could be worse on the old extended O'Neil family front.

I was curious if other people's MAGA/Fox News families have been taking precautions throughout the pandemic or not or if maybe they've changed their tunes recently. Since polls are dumb I decided to gather the only type of information I trust which is anecdotal *Hell World* readers' stories. Here's what people told me.

- I've been able to convince the Fox family members in California to wear them, but no luck with the ones who are also on Facebook.

- My parents are MAGA . . . they've been skeptics, but they have also taken it seriously enough to achieve the illusion of plausible deniability. They were in Florida from January to May, and my dad assured me that, unlike lazy, profligate, and diseased liberal blue states, Florida was run with hyper-competence. I know they wore masks on the plane back, but I doubt they wear them otherwise. And now my mom insists Florida only seems to have a problem because of "more testing."

- The Arizona MAGA family finally thinks it might get them and not just the "inner city people on the east coast." No masks, they just stay home. Being an antisocial loser is the original social distance strategy.

- My stepdad is MAGA. He sneers at the thought of wearing a mask, and does not practice social distancing, but does wear a mask grudgingly to go in stores when required. Last week he landed in the hospital for a tick-related disease. Now that he's compromised it will be interesting to see if his attitude changes or if his death wish continues. Sadly I don't have much hope. It's like they all drank the same mind-control poison and are following a flute song.

- One of my coworkers who listens to Rush Limbaugh in the office every day was freaking out about how nobody is taking Covid seriously anymore, and she doesn't understand how people can be so irresponsible.

- My Californian MAGA parents are extremely anti-lockdown measures of any kind. My dad has likened the mask requirements to the "mark of the beast" if you're familiar with Biblical stuff.

- My dad, a doctor who wears a mask literally every day of his professional life, has been going super hard in the paint with the anti-mask rhetoric. I can't even bring up the topic anymore without getting a stern discussion about "the facts."

- The pandemic has been an interesting paradox for my relatives in central Massachusetts who are both Trumpians and Preppers, but so far they're taking it very seriously.

- My mother-in-law lives in rural Ohio and has some of the brain rot. My husband was talking to her about our baby's first birthday and how we were doing a Zoom call because we can't see people in person, and she said something about how "It's not as bad here" and he goes "I'm looking at your chart right now and it's going up in Ohio" and she goes "Oh that's just Cleveland/Cincinnati." She had a friend over at her house at the time. I don't know if she wears a mask but I get the feeling she just goes with the flow of her friends and neighbors.

- Yes my family take it seriously. They're in a small city in Kansas of 50,000 people. They were totally not on board until a couple weeks back. There were a handful of cases, and then the city started hitting multiple days of record numbers of new cases for the entire state. My dad is now lambasting non-mask wearers on Facebook constantly. There's a big "wave two" energy which has gotten through to a lot of folks in this area. I think seeing stuff have to shut back down has been a wake up. The opening read as "it's all done," and the shutdowns are like "oh fuck I guess it isn't."

- My MAGA family are wearing masks, but they're also bitching about how the Democrats didn't do anything for Covid relief. They say if it wasn't for Trump people wouldn't even have the extra $600 a week, which they happily collected while their jobs were closed, but are now bitching about how it should never be extended because people need to be working. They're failing to grasp the fact that there really aren't many jobs to be working at right now, and because something doesn't impact them RIGHT NOW, no one should benefit. So yeah, typical MAGA logic.

- My family in Florida is a mix. They do masks, inconsistently, and acknowledge that social distance measures are a fine idea, but they also think no one in power has done anything wrong. "We can't just stop the economy." They visit my sickly grandma regularly.

- My Fox News dad in hella red, UBER MAGA upper-peninsula Michigan told me this entire thing was a hoax to defeat Trump. Then a month went by and he had my lil bros teach him Instacart and he hasn't left his house since April except to walk the dog. A pandemic is the antidote to some cases of brain worms it seems.

- My father did at first, then the GOP misinformation machine convinced him not to. "Let's kill off the boomers who vote for us in droves" is a weird strategy to be honest.

- Mine are just barely. They're still going out, but masking up more often than not. They're in South Carolina. Mom and sister went back to work a few weeks ago, but then mom retired, and now my sister is home sick. So . . . fingers crossed. Not sure what tipped them over besides two sons in the northeast and one very liberal friend.

- The MAGA corner of my family, located in the Midwest, has been isolating and taking this seriously from the beginning. One of them spent quite a bit of time and resources sewing masks and sending them to people in her circle. It probably helped that they had proof it wasn't a hoax as one member caught it on the job as a pharmacist. The employer did not provide PPE.

- My MAGA in-laws in Virginia are super serious about masks because my mother-in-law has a lung problem. My MAGA brother and sister-in-law in Texas have so far refused to wear them.

- My mom doesn't watch Fox News, but she's a huge Trump supporter, and she's taking it very seriously. I've been incredibly surprised.

- At first my parents on Long Island were buying the Fox bullshit. Now they're in this confusion zone where they are aghast at all the people taking no precautions but also very angry at "government overreach."

- My chud-adjacent dad is a truck driver who hauls medical waste and wasn't being supplied PPE. The man owns multiple shirts from the Reagan museum, but would probably deck someone inside without a mask as this point.

- My dad, a retired surgeon and Trump voter, is heavily pro-mask. I think what's interesting is the best path to getting the right on board with masks might be to tell them, "Hey, COVID-19 isn't a big deal. You'll be fine as long as you wear a mask!" which supports their feelings that it's "exaggerated" but makes it conditional on mask wearing.

- Somehow one I'm related to in Connecticut both takes the lockdown seriously—maybe because there's no alternative here?— and thinks it's a Democrat hoax/lie/overblown or whatever Tucker or Crowder is saying that night.

- No. Sadly. My Fox-addicted family member in Maine thinks it is all overblown. It's breaking my heart. Refuses to wear a mask. Rants like crazy about it.

SOMETIMES THE TRUTH TAKES A SIDE

"Since American journalism's pivot many decades ago from an openly partisan press to a model of professed objectivity, the mainstream has allowed what it considers objective truth to be decided almost exclusively by white reporters and their mostly white bosses," Wesley Lowery the two-time Pulitzer-winning reporter wrote in the *New York Times* in June.

"And those selective truths have been calibrated to avoid offending the sensibilities of white readers. On opinion pages, the contours of acceptable public debate have largely been determined through the gaze of white editors."

I called Lowery to talk about the ideas in that piece and the overabundance of deference given to police by media outlets as well as the ongoing idiotic debate about "cancel culture" in the media.

IT WAS YOUR BIRTHDAY THE OTHER DAY?
Yeah two days back. My days are all blurred together with coronavirus brain.

I HEARD YOU TURNED THIRTY, SO ON BEHALF OF ALL OF US OVER FORTY WITH ZERO PULITZERS I WOULD LIKE TO INVITE YOU TO GO AND FUCK YOURSELF.

Well I tell myself that every day too, so don't worry about it!

I REALLY DON'T WANT TO KEEP THE CONVERSATION GOING ABOUT THE GODDAMN HARPER'S "CANCEL CULTURE" LETTER, BUT IT DOES TIE INTO SOME OF THE STUFF YOU'VE BEEN TALKING ABOUT LATELY. WHAT ARE YOUR THOUGHTS ON THE DEBATE ABOUT "CANCEL CULTURE" IN GENERAL WE'RE HAVING NOW?

I don't like the term cancel culture. I find it to be pretty meaningless, in part because as long as there has been an American culture there have been some views that are seen as outside the mainstream, and people have faced recrimination for expressing them. To be clear, most often the victims of that type of pressure are not people like the signatories, but are, in fact, Black people, or other minorities, native people, immigrants, Muslims, communists . . . Typically not white, very well-platformed centrists types.

But beyond that, there's a fallacy sometimes in this conversation, where many of the signatories of a letter like this would also assert that one of the ways to combat what they would consider to be bad speech would be additional speech. But the very thing they are upset about is people exercising speech: people sending a bunch of tweets at them saying they suck, or writing a column saying they shouldn't receive commissions to write any columns because they suck. All of those things are people's speech rights, and I think that's important.

I think two things can be true at the same time. It is important for the leaders of our institutions to operate from a position of what is the right decision to make versus what is the wrong decision, and not always be swayed . . . "Everyone's mad on the internet right now so I need to do something" decisions get made that way all the time. I think we see that in terms of some of the overreactions. To be clear, this still happens more often to Black people or radical leftists or women than it does to the types of people that the signatories are. It's also true that there are cases where there's institutional overreaction. Secondarily, a lot of these folks are people that have held a monopoly on the marketplace of ideas and are suddenly in a world that is more diverse and where speech is more democratized, where everyone can have a Twitter account. Some of what these folks are reacting to is criticism of their speech. Suddenly they face reputational recrimination because their ideas are bad. And they're going "This is unfair, it's the end of democracy!"

I COMPARE IT TO THE POLICE. THEY'RE NOT JUST CONTENT HAVING A MONOPOLY ON THE ABILITY TO WIELD VIOLENCE AND POWER, THEY ALSO HAVE TO FRAME THEMSELVES AS BEING VICTIMS UNDER SIEGE ALL THE TIME.

Correct. They're the victims of the story. But two things can be true. If someone is fired or run out of a job unfairly that does matter. Individual circumstances do matter. But we're seeing this strategic wielding of circumstances and grouping of incidents that don't even fit together, or aren't even being described honestly, so that a group of people who feel as if they are losing collective power can frame themselves as, not only the victims, but the brave warriors on behalf of freedom and democracy. It's like, no, people saying they don't like your work and that you're bad at it is not a crisis of speech.

ONE THING THAT BOTHERS ME IS THE FRAMING OF IT BEING SOMETHING COMING EXCLUSIVELY FROM THE LEFT. YOU KNOW THIS PROBABLY BETTER THAN I DO, BUT EVEN JUST AS A FREELANCER AT NEWSPAPERS AND MAGAZINES, EVERY SINGLE ARTICLE YOU WRITE THERE ARE PEOPLE IN THE COMMENTS OR WRITING EMAILS TRYING TO SNITCH ON YOU FOR THIS OR THAT.

Of course. Right-wing people have been trying to get me fired every day of my career. I don't recall any brave collective efforts on behalf of my speech rights.

I DON'T KNOW IF IN YOUR TIME AT THE *WASHINGTON POST* IF ANYONE SAID EXPLICITLY, OR IS IT JUST SOMETHING THAT IS UNDERSTOOD INSTITUTIONALLY, THAT A BLACK PERSON IS GOING TO ALWAYS ALREADY BE UNABLE TO REPORT ON CERTAIN ISSUES OBJECTIVELY?

I don't know that it's something explicitly stated. It's more about the environment and culture and assumptions made by bosses and editors in how they assign stories and in edits they make. Again this goes back to power. Something I talk about all the time. What we know is that even in a moment when more people of more backgrounds have platforms and the ability to talk in public, largely due to social media, the people who control the most powerful platforms in our broad press remain a very specific type of person. They have such power in this space. So I don't think it's something that's stated all the time, but it shows up and is manifested in coverage, in the way people are treated, in terms of how assignments are handed out, in terms of hiring.

Something people say to me all the time is you just want all journalism to make decisions the way you would. To have *your* morals and ethics. That's not necessarily true. I think journalism has like 98 percent someone's else's morals and ethics and 2 percent mine. Would I love to have a little more of mine? Of course. But what I argue for is a more deliberate process that acknowledges that there are morals and ethics at all. All these folks get off on saying "We don't make any decisions ever. This is what it's always been" as a way of shielding the fact that they are constantly making decisions, and those decisions are subject to their biases.

THE FIRST THING I SAID WHEN I STARTED MY NEWSLETTER WAS THAT I PROMISE NOT TO HEAR BOTH SIDES. MOST STORIES ARE NOT GRAY. LIFE ISN'T A PRESTIGE HBO DRAMA. THERE ARE GOOD GUYS AND BAD GUYS IN EVERY STORY. THERE ARE THE POWERFUL FORCES OF CAPITALISM, OR THE DEFENDERS OF CAPITALISM LIKE THE POLICE ON ONE SIDE, AND THEN THERE ARE THOSE BEING GROUND UP IN THE GEARS. I AM MUCH MORE CONCERNED ABOUT THE LATTER THAN THE JUSTIFICATIONS FOR WHY THE POWERFUL PEOPLE ARE HURTING THEM. YOU COULDN'T WALK INTO A NEWSPAPER FOR AN INTERVIEW AND SAY THAT AND GET A JOB RIGHT?

Sure, but what I think that misses is that in a newsroom there's a need for all different types of people, including a need for someone like you. In the world where I'm running a newsroom . . . I do think part of the role of the mainstream press is to make powerful people and institutions be confronted by less powerful people. To pose to them hard questions.

To ask the senator something they would otherwise not be asked. We are supposed to be an equalizer of power, and to bring ideas and perspectives into places where they otherwise would not be. In our society that means confronting Jeff Bezos about how he treats his workers. In a world in which someone walks in and says I want to stand up for the little guy, the idea that that would ban them from working in respectable journalism, to me, I think is kind of [crazy].

But look, I don't think we have to change our conversations about rigor, about standards. I think all that stuff is really important.

I AGREE. WHEN I SAY THAT I AM 100 PERCENT BIASED IN MY WRITING THAT DOESN'T MEAN I'M GOING TO LIE OR MAKE THINGS UP. YOU DON'T NEED TO EXAGGERATE THE DETAILS OF CORRUPTION OR WORKER ABUSE OR WHATEVER BECAUSE THEY'RE ALREADY BAD ENOUGH. THERE'S NO NEED FOR FABULISM.

I think about this all the time. If a story is that stunning or insane you can write it with the calmest language. If the facts themselves are ridiculous you don't have to write it up at all. You can just list the true things.

BUT DON'T YOU ALSO THINK YOU CAN PRESENT SOMETHING HORRIFIC IN A NEUTERED LANGUAGE THAT DRAINS THE BLOOD FROM IT? ESPECIALLY WITH THE *TIMES* . . .

I certainly think that happens. Some of that is about pulling punches, not actually writing down the true things. But the way we do sourcing, the way we allow people sometimes to rebut allegations against them in the same sentences where we are saying what the allegation is . . . These are decisions that are made in the writing and editing process. It's less about the individual reporter than the structure of how our journalism works. Fairness is important. You call everyone, you talk to them and hear what they say, but at the end of the day we have to write what we believe.

THE *TIMES* IS SO BAD AT THIS AND EVERYONE COMPLAINS ABOUT IT CONSTANTLY. THE OTHER DAY THE HEADLINE WAS LIKE "TRUMP'S LATEST RACE-BASED APPEAL TO WHITE VOTERS DEFENDING THE CONFEDERATE FLAG . . ." YOU'VE BEEN IN HIGHER LEVEL POSITIONS THAN ME, ARE THERE PEOPLE OPERATING AT THE *POST* OR *THE BOSTON GLOBE* OR WHATEVER SAYING "WHY DON'T WE JUST CALL HIM A RACIST?" OR . . .

I'll be honest, in my experience there is far less discussion than there should be. Everything operates on autopilot. So often these things that become national conversations are things almost no one talked about in the first place. We know this. We know James Bennett didn't read the Tom Cotton article. You see these examples time and again where the upshot isn't even institutional cowardice, or a deliberate decision to water anything down, it's that they never even had the conversation on what to do. So some person, the copywriter who slapped the headline on, some person in the bureaucracy of journalism, made a small decision without any weight to it, it got thrust on the internet, and moments later it's a whole thing. To be clear, that is not to suggest were our newsrooms not more diverse that more of those decisions would not go this way. But it's also to say I think a lot of this stuff has to slow down and there has to be real conversation about this issue. And those conversations would be served by having Black and Brown people in the room in the first place. Or people who aren't convinced that the worst thing that can happen to someone is to be called a racist. Look man, we all have prejudices and have to combat them. The idea that someone would say something racist, to most Black Americans is just like how a Monday works. Meanwhile white people are like "We're locked in the massive battle, can we call Trump's tweet racist?" It's like, well, was it racist? Then call it that.

Whether or not it's appropriate for the *Post* or *Times* to call, insert whatever statement, racist, is a subjective decision. If you got one hundred people you might have one hundred different points on the scale where they draw the line. Some of them might be grouped together, but there would be cases like, ok this one yes, maybe not that one. Even people of the same politics. I think we have to acknowledge it is a subjective decision, and so therefore who should be involved in making that decision? Should a group of white guys be talking about whether or not it's racist to talk about crime-infested and rat-infested Baltimore, or perhaps should a Black person be involved. Not even one Black person, many. I think that's the structural failing in most of our newsrooms, that we have a presidential administration and prior to that a campaign that has nakedly played on white racial grievance. Explicitly. There are stories where Steve Bannon talked about why they did this and how they did this. It's not even an accusation against them, it's a fact.

AND WE'RE SEEING IT NOW. TRUMP IS SOMEHOW LEANING ON IT EVEN MORE IN THE LEAD UP TO THE ELECTION.

Certainly. What we have now is the decision makers charged with telling us the truth haven't even done the reading, so they don't know what they're looking at. They have no expertise on these issues, and they are the arbiters of whether or not something crosses the line. They literally don't have the academic expertise, and they also don't have the expertise of being Black or Brown in America. Which is an expertise. Like you said, I think that's a failure. What's hard is that there have been so many generations and decades of white guy editors training the next generation of white guy editors who are now training the next generation of white guy and white women editors . . . And here we are today and they're all going, "Call something racist? We could never do that!" when every Black person is like, "That was racist." It's become so normative in the industry that it seems like it's the way it's supposed to be as opposed to a decision that's made.

SO MUCH OF JOURNALISM SEEMS LIKE THIS PRIM UPPER-CLASS CRISIS OF MANNERS TYPE OF THING. "WELL, THAT'S SIMPLY NOT DONE!" I THINK PEOPLE FORGET ALL THIS SHIT IS MADE UP. WE JUST MADE UP THESE STANDARDS. JOURNALISM WASN'T PASSED DOWN FROM GOD ON A STONE TABLET. IT'S JUST A PROFESSIONAL GROUP'S INTERNAL STANDARDS. THOSE CAN CHANGE. BUT THERE'S SO MUCH RESISTANCE TO THAT, ESPECIALLY WITH THE IDEA OF OBJECTIVITY.
ONE THING YOU WROTE IN THE TIMES THE OTHER DAY I LIKED: "NEUTRAL OBJECTIVITY TRIPS OVER ITSELF TO FIND WAYS TO AVOID TELLING THE TRUTH. NEUTRAL OBJECTIVITY INSISTS WE USE CLUNKY EUPHEMISMS LIKE 'OFFICER-INVOLVED SHOOTING.'"

I FEEL LIKE OBJECTIVITY IS A FORM OF LYING TO PEOPLE. WOULD YOU GO THAT FAR?

One of the things that's difficult here is you have objectivity, what the word actually means, then the way it is too often applied in newsrooms. The neutral part of that is important, because there are any number of things where you can read my writing and not think that it's neutral. If I'm writing about a murder, that story should probably not come across as neutral about the murder. Clearly the murder was bad! You still have to fair to the person accused of the murder, because maybe they didn't do it. There's all sorts of nuances. But the piece itself, you should not walk away going, that was a really neutral piece about the murder.

RIGHT DOWN THE MIDDLE!

I think sometimes in the journalism conversation we miss this because it's a decision we've made that we pretend isn't even a decision. There is someone out there who might argue that in fact the murder was good. I could find you a person. But it is a moral decision to say murder is bad. It is not neutral.

I GUESS IT DEPENDS ON WHO IS GETTING MURDERED.

Sure. It's not bad that objectivity means telling the truth and being fair, of course we should do that, but the extent to which we want a theoretical reader to feel as if we have not taken any side on anything. Sometimes the truth takes a side. The truth is not in fact neutral. That does not remove the nuance of stories, that there aren't other interesting angles or complexities. But there are many times where we do journalism and we stumble upon a truth. There is a good guy and a bad guy here. Or a good action or a bad action, it's not even about the person themselves. Did they do something that should not have been done? It's our job to say that. And it's not our job to now allow the things we write to suggest there is legitimate debate over things where there is none. We saw this with climate change coverage for example. We went on and on for so long giving platforms to people who are denying basic science. That slowed the nation and therefore the world's ability to address a crisis, because we concealed the truth from readers through our stylistic decisions.

THAT JOURNALISTIC CONVENTION VERY WELL MAY SPELL THE END OF THE WORLD. BACK TO THE TERM "OFFICER-INVOLVED SHOOTING." IS THAT SOMETHING THAT YOU THINK IS A REFLEXIVE STANDARD WAY OF DOING THINGS IN NEWSPAPERS, OR DO YOU SEE THAT AS AN EXPLICIT DECISION BEING MADE TO BE DEFERENTIAL TO THE POLICE AT ALL TIMES WITHIN INSTITUTIONS?

I think it's an institutional reflex. One of the things to remember is that reflex is informed by history. In so much of the modern newspaper era, not necessarily every newspaper, but in most local metro newspapers where they were competing with two or three other dailies through most of their history, one of the best thing you could do was slap a big sexy headline on the front page with the grizzliest details of the crime of the day. That would be the thing the paperboys were yelling out. So it was extremely important to cultivate police sources, and therefore a structure that is deferential to the police and their narratives. They are the key source, the people providing the information. That coverage itself relies solely on their willingness to provide that information. What that did over the course of generations was create a situation in which, too often, the coverage reads like it could've been written by the police themselves. In large part because it doesn't have the appropriate skepticism for what the police are saying, nor does it take time to be fair to other people in the story. The police say this guy did a crime, and we're going to throw them on the front page of the paper, having reached this guy or not. We're going to throw in his entire criminal history, despite the fact that we haven't even gotten the records yet. We haven't talked to the lawyers in those cases. We haven't gotten the trial transcripts. We don't actually know what happened in those cases. We just know what either the police are telling us, or "a search of the docket says XYZ."

RIGHT. IT'S SO RARE THAT YOU HEAR FIRSTHAND FROM THE SUSPECT IN THE ORIGINAL REPORTING ON IT, OR EVEN THEIR LAWYER.

And that original reporting colors the public perception of what has happened. You can never put that back. And by the way, the jurors in that person's case are theoretically reading that article.

I like the comparison of journalists to referees and umpires calling balls and strikes. An umpire can never suggest that they don't influence the game. They fundamentally control the game. The difference between the ball and the strike, a subjective decision, can cost someone the World Series, right? Are the umpires the star of the game? No. Do they have their name on their jersey? No. Would we like it to be interchangeable who the umpire is? Yes. But we know that that's not true. We understand the umpire matters and that the way they call balls and strikes changes the outcome of the game.

I THINK THE RIGHT UNDERSTANDS THAT BETTER, AND THEY PLAY THE REFS ALL THE TIME. LIKE HOW IN A GAME YOU GET A MAKEUP CALL. THE REF DIDN'T CALL HOLDING ON ONE PLAY SO THEY GET THE TEAM BACK FOR IT BY CALLING IT AGAINST THE OTHER TEAM TO MAKE IT SEEM LIKE HE'S BEING FAIR. BUT WHAT'S ACTUALLY HAPPENED IS TWO WRONGS HAVE BEEN DONE. THEY DIDN'T SEE THE FIRST PENALTY, SO NOW THEY INVENT ONE THAT DIDN'T EXIST TO CREATE THE IDEA THAT THEY'RE NOT MANIPULATING THINGS. THE RIGHT KNOWS THAT VERY WELL, THAT MEDIA INSTITUTIONS ARE SUSCEPTIBLE TO THAT.

Of course. And they're getting played by these people without even realizing it. What you end up doing is eroding the legitimacy of the entire system.

EXACTLY. OBVIOUSLY YOU'RE A GREAT REPORTER, AND I'VE READ YOUR STUFF FOR A WHILE, BUT THE REASON I WANTED TO TALK TO YOU NOW IS IT SEEMS LIKE YOU'VE DEVELOPED A REAL RED ASS AGAINST BOSSES IN THE MEDIA. HOW DID YOU COME BY THAT REDDENING ASS?

I think I've always had a longstanding beef with authority and rules. But part of it has been, I kind of exist in a different ecosystem now, at least in this exact moment. I'm working at CBS as a correspondent for this *60 Minutes* spinoff. It's kind of understood that *60 Minutes* correspondents are individual people. No one is like, "Anderson Cooper this tweet is over the line." It's a different world than being a newspaper reporter where it's understood you are supposed to be this company person who has no beliefs about anything. I've always kind of flirted with that line a little bit, but there's been something freeing about this moment to be able to speak out and speak out in ways that are different.

I'll also say there is something about doing the work that empowers you to make the criticism. I want to do good journalism. I care about that more than anything else. When I talk about these things it's because I wish the institutions would fix them so I never have to talk about them again. I don't think it would be fun to be an ombudsman or media critic. I would like us to hire some Black people so I don't have to be like "Hey can we hire some Black people?" ever again.

A decade into my professional career, what's the point of having put in all that work, and gained some standing, if I'm unwilling to use that platform and credibility that comes with that to try to agitate for a better industry? What's the point of having a platform at all if you don't use it to try to make things better?

WELL YOU'RE SUPPOSED TO GET YOURS, THEN PULL UP THE LADDER AND FUCK EVERYONE ELSE.

Exactly. I always go back to my roots in the Black journalism world. I say there are seventeen Black journalists and we've all dated each other. Everyone knows everyone. Because of that there's always been the sense of . . . there are older Black journalists who I could not have done anything in my career without their help and guidance and mentorship.

So I foundationally and fundamentally see that as my responsibility.

I don't have the desire to be a partisan political figure. Even though I get my tweets off sometimes. The things I tweet about are journalism. And what is the point of being a big prominent journalism public figure to not then weigh in on journalism and how it should operate?

I also know this is an industry that is unforgiving. And it's changed very rapidly. I don't take for granted that today I have a platform and tomorrow I might not.

YOU MIGHT GET CANCELED!

Right! And again I'm actually at risk of getting canceled. The *Washington Post* tried to cancel me. I've seen so many generations of Black journalists chewed up and spit out by this field, and look, I'm still relatively young, I don't think I want to be doing this shit when I'm sixty, so I might as well put my foot on the scale as much as possible so it changes for the people coming up behind me.

LIKE ASKING ME TO TAKE THAT BULLET HOME TO MY OWN FAMILY

Richard Rose died of complications related to Covid on July 4. A thirty-seven-year-old veteran from Ohio his <u>family said</u> he was "active in helping homeless vets and in preventing veteran suicide."

The reason why his death is notable the reason why we know about it in the first place among all the tens of thousands of other deaths is because he's gone posthumously viral for something he posted back in April on Facebook. "Let's make this clear," he wrote. "I'm not buying a mask. I've made it this far by not buying into that damn hype."

It's funny but it's not. Or maybe it is I don't know.

When I saw one of the many tweets going around yesterday dunking on him I shared it myself my gut instinct at the time being fuck this fucking reckless asshole who knows how many other people he might have infected.

Naturally many of the people laughing at his death have turned him into a MAGA caricature but after reading through his Facebook that doesn't really seem to be the case he seems like he was a more complicated person than that occasionally posting about gay rights and arresting abusive police and so on. I'm not sure why that matters but I guess it does. Maybe it doesn't. I don't know. Mostly the whole thing makes me feel sad at the moment and angrier at the president and our other idiot leaders and the denialist media who have convinced people like Rose that this is all a hoax. He should have known better sure but there are so many people constantly lying to us so professionally and without shame is it any wonder that a lot of people are going to believe them? Either way he did not have to die. None of these people had to die.

"We were blown away, you know? You hear about this virus and you don't expect it to affect people, younger people like ourselves," Nick Conley his friend told Cleveland 19 News.

"Rick is getting slaughtered online right now for his decision that he made not to wear a mask and that's not right," he said.

Is it? I don't know. This is going to become a more regular occurrence I imagine. People who were pandemic deniers are going to die and their old posts are going to circulate and we'll all go lol . . . and then we'll go wait . . . :(

"We should still be compassionate whether we agree with someone's beliefs or not. Someone has passed away and we should have some compassion towards that," he said.

Should we? I honestly don't know.

I just read this story from News 4 San Antonio about a patient in their thirties who died at a hospital there. In it Chief Medical Officer of Methodist Healthcare Dr. Jane Appleby said one of her patients died after going to a Covid party and I don't know if I necessarily believe that that is a real thing but who knows. I don't know.

"Just before the patient died, they looked at their nurse and said 'I think I made a mistake, I thought this was a hoax, but it's not,'" Appleby said and that seems a little too good to be true so maybe I don't believe that either but maybe I do who knows.

What do you imagine happening when you imagine yourself getting it? I imagine it sucking real bad shit but at the same time I envision a full staff of medical professionals working night and day tirelessly to save my specific ass but that is because I am a white able-bodied cis straight male who naturally and instinctually expects no cost to be spared when it comes to saving my life because my life is obviously valuable. Logically and rationally I know that's not how it works but I still believe it anyway even though as I've written many times that when I go to the doctor for one of my recurring chronic injury issues they fuck around for like five minutes staring at a clipboard while I sit there with a cold ass on the cold paper they pull over the cold bed and say something like uh I don't know what to tell you bud then peace out because my pain is not their problem. It's their job but not their problem which is different.

I just read a thread on Twitter by a user named @chronicparent30 about our expectations around being saved if we catch the Covid that I found illuminating.

"So I want to share something. I talked to my therapist about my cautiousness with Covid and how all the ableds around me are acting like I'm over exaggerating. She pointed out something that feels obvious but I hadn't actually consciously realized . . . All these people (ableds) are speaking about this virus as a hypothetical scenario. They are naive to the reality of being hospitalized and facing their own mortality. They can't fully conceptualize it because they haven't experienced it. I have. Many disabled people have."

"Also they are used to living in a body that doesn't let them down. A body that recovers easily from illness and probably doesn't get ill very often—that is not my baseline assumption about my own disabled body because it's not been my experience at all."

"And lastly, they operate under an assumption that if they were to contract it the medical professionals would do everything they can. They've not had traumatizing medical experiences like I have. They've not been ill for years and had doctors give zero shits . . . Their baseline assumption is that doctors can and will fix things. That again has not been my experience. Also goes without saying they don't have all the fears of being disabled in this pandemic and thus seen as expendable—an opinion legitimized by our government."

Here's a question I had about the deployment of federal troops into our cities after they first arrived in Portland in July: How does one know the unidentified camouflaged army man snatching you and putting you in a random van isn't just a militia guy and what penalties do you face for defending yourself in that situation?

I am certain that you would face some obscene charges for assaulting a federal agent. Seems like a real bad deal man!

Unless you're a military cosplayer serial killer who loves to kidnap people I guess. It's probably a good turn of events for them. Those guys never catch a break.

Apparently it's a good question legally speaking because the state of Oregon is now suing the Trump administration for the "kidnap and false arrest" of protestors in the state. As Tim Dickinson in *Rolling Stone* explained:

"In a harrowing new tactic, reminiscent of fascist regimes, armed federal officers without agency badges have begun grabbing protesters off the street, throwing them into unmarked cars, and jailing them without formally arresting them, according to court records. The state of Oregon is seeking a permanent injunction to prevent what it alleges are violations of the Fourth Amendment's protections against 'unreasonable seizures' and the Fifth Amendment's guarantees of due process."

"Ordinarily, a person exercising his right to walk through the streets of Portland who is confronted by anonymous men in military-type fatigues and ordered into an unmarked van can reasonably assume that he is being kidnapped and is the victim of a crime," Oregon Attorney General Ellen Rosenblum argues in the suit.

"Defendants are injuring the occupants of Portland by taking away citizens' ability to determine whether they are being kidnapped by militia or other malfeasants dressed in paramilitary gear (such that they may engage in self-defense to the fullest extent permitted by law) or are being arrested (such that resisting might amount to a crime)."

It's July and the president is now sending forces to Chicago and probably other cities soon and spending millions of dollars on ads aimed at scaring people into thinking noted Maoist Joe Biden is going to abolish the police and the suburbs and leave old ladies to fend for themselves when Antifa come to the steal their liver medicine. I don't think the next couple months are going to be "good" buddy. Probably not very good at all.

I read a piece in *The New York Times* I quite liked well not liked but you know what I mean. It's by a teacher explaining why she doesn't feel safe going back to work which is an outlook I am rather familiar with living as I do with a teacher who doesn't feel safe going back to work.

"Every day when I walk into work as a public-school teacher, I am prepared to take a bullet to save a child. In the age of school shootings, that's what the job requires. But asking me to return to the classroom amid a pandemic and expose myself and my family to COVID-19 is like asking me to take that bullet home to my own family."

"I won't do it, and you shouldn't want me to."

It's a fine piece overall but man that sentence there ". . . like asking me to take that bullet home to my own family." Jesus.

Mark Berman of the *Washington Post* shared the article and <u>asked a question</u> I can't get out of my head now either. ". . . How are you supposed to do active shooting drills that involve teaching kids to huddle together out of sight if schools do reopen with social distancing rules?"

No crying when the shooter comes in kids you might get your Covid tears on your classmates.

HE BASICALLY TOLD ME IF YOU DON'T LIKE IT QUIT

It's August and I spoke to an employee at a water park in Florida about how unseriously customers and his employer are taking safety measures and how badly things in the state are in general.

SO YOUR SITUATION AT WORK IS PRETTY FUCKED UP?

Yeah I work at a rinky-dink water park and there's no social distancing, it's terrible, but most people are still going to work around here. I have a friend who works at Walgreens and nothing changed. She works five days a week getting screamed at by old assholes not wearing masks. She didn't even get to do the lockdown thing. I got laid off for a couple months.

They laid us all off via email on March 15. Then they called me two weeks before Memorial Day and offered me my job back with the implicit if you don't come back we will hire someone to fill your slot . . . They also hired us all back as seasonal workers, so no vision or dental insurance anymore, even though those things sucked.

I used to have to climb the towers every morning to turn the slides on and I'd have to push down the urge to jump off, and that was before Covid. Now I work mid-shifts so I almost never have to climb the towers, but fuck man.

JESUS MAN. THAT'S AWFUL. I'M SORRY. AND THEY EXPLICITLY TOLD YOU IF YOU DON'T COME BACK YOU'RE GONNA LOSE YOUR JOB?

I asked do we have to come back? They said you don't have to if the virus makes you feel unsafe, but we can't hold your job forever. I'm the only person there that does what I do so if they replace me . . . We've had other people that didn't come back and they replaced them. So I came back even though I was making more money on unemployment, and I make like $5 more an hour than most of the other employees.

WERE YOU GETTING THE FULL UNEMPLOYMENT PLUS ENHANCED?

Yeah I was getting the Florida maximum, like $225 a week, plus the $600, which is definitely more than I make. I had the most money in my bank account I've ever had in my entire life in the beginning of May.

AND THAT'S SMART. WATERPARKS DO NOT NEED TO BE OPEN DURING A PANDEMIC.

No they do not. I even had a sit down with the general manager where I told him I felt like the Covid rules they implemented were a joke and I cried. He basically told me if you don't like it quit.

Right when I came back they said we're going to do all this social distancing stuff, we're gonna be safe, blah blah blah. They had these big plans for social distancing and masks and whatnot.

I came back and realized that almost all of it was for show. I was talking with the guy who wrote our Covid response. I asked about the basic premise. Why is it we need to open? He said, well, we have employees that I've had to personally drive to the grocery store and buy groceries for them because they can't get their unemployment. We have a responsibility to offer them employment so they can work and make money and feed their kids. I was like, oh so you're basically Superman and Mother Teresa mixed together. You're so nice for giving people the opportunity to make $10 an hour cleaning toilets.

HE FRAMED IT LIKE THEY WERE DOING THIS ALTRUISTIC THING?

When I had the meeting with the GM when I was basically crying in front of him he said, well, we're not going to be making money, we're not gonna set any records, we have to offer people the opportunity to have fun and offer the employees the opportunity to make money. But we're the busiest we've ever been, and I think we are making money, because we're packed every day. The other parks are still closed.

YOU SAID THEY HIRED YOU BACK AND TOOK AWAY SOME OF YOUR BENEFITS?

When I originally got hired it was as a full-time employee. They decided to hire everybody back as seasonal. I think I might be able to stay on full time, but because they classified us as seasonal they don't have to offer us vision and dental so they don't anymore. I paid into it just long enough to get the ability to go get my teeth cleaned and get glasses, and then I got laid off a week later.

DO YOU GET NORMAL HEALTH INSURANCE?

I mean yeah, but it sucks. I almost never use it because it's expensive and doesn't cover much. Like everyone else in the world. Or America anyway. Today the GM got back from a two-week precautionary Covid quarantine and he came up to me to ask how I was doing and I mentioned the dental and vision thing and he suggested that I go to Mexico to get all my teeth pulled and replaced on the cheap.

WAIT WHAT. WAS THAT SERIOUS OR A JOKE?

I told him the reason I took the job is I wanted to be able to fix my teeth. He's seen I have a couple teeth missing. He said go down to Corpus Christi and for like five grand they'll just yank them all out. I was like, I don't know man, that seems drastic. It's a thing I've heard people suggest to people without a lot of money. I'm thirty-nine. I know people younger than me that have had all their teeth pulled and replaced because their teeth were so bad.

SO NOW THAT YOU'RE OPEN THE SAFETY STANDARDS ARE A JOKE?

They play this thing on the announcement twice an hour saying "Social distancing . . . stay six feet away from anyone who's not in your family . . . Stay on the little dots." But people are standing in line right next to each other on the towers. The wave pool is packed with people. The customers aren't doing social distancing because we don't have anyone that enforces it. That would require walking up to people and having an argument about it. It's the same thing with the masks, it's like, well, everyone is outside, and you can't wear a mask when you're in the water cause you'll drown . . . So we tell the customers it's recommended but you don't have to, and literally nobody does it. I have a mask on all day and all the other employees do. It's like, if we're all wearing masks that's cool, but why are we wearing a mask? Oh yeah the customers might have it and they're not wearing a mask. It seems so obvious to say if you're not actively eating or in the water to put a mask on. It would be such an easy thing to do. But it would also require us to tell all our customers to do something they don't want to do.

I go into the grocery store and people are wearing masks. But it's so crazy, I go into work and there's the part of my brain that's like wear a mask! but no one is, and I have to be cool. I can't freak out. I'm not allowed to walk up to random customers and say what the fuck is wrong with you?

IT MUST BE TEMPTING.
Well yeah.

ARE THE PEOPLE THAT COME THERE LOCALS?
The bosses seem to think they're all locals but that's absurd. Anybody within sixty or a hundred miles who wants to swim in a water park, we're one of the few places open. So we get a lot of people who think it's a good idea to travel to Florida to have fun because I guess the virus isn't happening here.

YEAH FLORIDA IS IMMUNE.

I went to the beach to see what was what, and there were so many people we were like never mind. It's honestly shocking how many people are at that beach. As far as the eye can see in every direction. I'm scared and furious and I feel like I have no control over anything.

I send the governor angry emails every day that have probably put me on some list.

DO YOU THINK DESANTIS FUCKED THINGS UP BAD?

Yeah. It's such a dumb thing to be like Trump, ugh, but I think the reason DeSantis didn't go all in on masks is because he didn't think he'd get reelected or that he'd get shit on by Trump. You'd prefer to have children die than get tweeted at by the president?

WHAT A COWARD. SO YOUR ROOMMATE IS SCARED OF YOU, YOU SAID?

She hasn't gone to work since March . . . Both of her parents in the last year had cancer and got better. She hasn't seen her family since March because she doesn't want to get them sick. And she's afraid to go to the grocery store. Then I go to work and I'm around a thousand naked people. I have a friend who I go hiking with occasionally, but she thinks that's a risk on top . . . Dude, I could go spit in her mouth and it would be more safe than me just going to work every day.

AND YOU'RE BEING FUCKED WITH BY YOUR LANDLORD?

They're running raffles like if you pay your rent early we'll put your name in a contest to win cash. Or sending us emails with links to the Florida job sites to find a job. Or ways to get the government to help you pay your rent if you can't pay on time. I understand it's their job to sit in an office and collect money from everyone once a month, but it's so filthy that he thinks sending out an email blast with some links . . . It's so tone deaf and shitty.

ARE YOU DOING CAPACITY LIMITS?

Yeah. We're at 50 percent capacity. I can't even imagine it being the real capacity. There would be so many human beings you wouldn't ever see the bottom of the pool. But we've hit half capacity sometimes and had to turn people away.

ARE THE CUSTOMERS ASSHOLES ABOUT IT?

Yeah, but I'm not over there at the admissions counter. But I've seen customers be absolute shitheads to employees over dumb shit. Arguing about coupons or whatever. It's like . . . come on. You're here to have fun, you're not here to cuss out sixteen year olds.

HAVE THERE BEEN ANY OUTBREAKS AT PARKS YOU'VE HEARD OF?

I've read stuff on Reddit about people who work at Disney saying there's a lot of people who have it and they're not telling the public. I don't know if that's real or not. We haven't had anyone test positive that I know of, or that they've told us about. Like I said, my friend works at Walgreens and three of the Walgreens in her area had people test positive and they didn't tell anyone.

WHAT WOULD YOU PREFER, TO SEE EVERYTHING SHUT DOWN AGAIN?

I hope the whole state closes back down because the numbers are terrifying. I don't like being on unemployment, but I also don't like going to a place that's hot as hell . . . I mean it sucks working at a water park without Covid. The sun's brutal, we're wearing polo shirts. But if I had my way and I could snap my fingers I'd tell the governor to close everything, send everyone home. Mail everyone a check. The end. So people don't die for no fucking reason.

IF YOU'RE AFRAID OF DYING,
AND YOU'RE HOLDING ON

I woke from a nightmare this morning and you were there and we were all there we were packed too tightly in a car about to head over the Bourne Bridge leaving Cape Cod and it was so so steep and the sky was so so blue and there were no barriers on either side of the bridge and I was sure we were going to careen over the edge into the water below but we didn't because I woke up and snapped back into all of this instead.

Maybe it was the hamburger. The cause of the nightmare I mean. We live very close to a McDonald's now so last night "as a bit" we decided to get food there for the first time in like ten years and then "as a bit" I ended up feeling gross and gray and grumpy about it almost immediately. This morning I feel like absolute shit but I think it has more to do with everything else rather than this one specific thing. I can't remember being this grumpy in a long time.

Hold on Michelle's mother and sister just arrived for an outdoor visit and I went outside and showed our niece the hole to the chipmunk tunnel that stretches underneath our driveway and that cheered me up for thirty seconds but now I'm back to miserable.

Before I went to get the food I tried calling ahead to order the hamburgs so as to reduce time inside and Michelle started laughing at me like what are you doing you don't call in to order ahead at McDonald's and sure enough the kid who answered said uhh we . . . can't do that so I walked over and ordered in person and the food was ready within thirty seconds anyway. It was just there waiting for me to show up the whole time.

Almost every day my new neighbor is outside grilling up piping hot burgs and/or dogs and one time I said hey man that smells real good and he offered me one but I was just about to eat a big meal we were making so I said I can't but definitely another time and he never offered again :(and I think I must have broken some unspoken ironclad Suburb Law shit there. I guess he thought I didn't want his burgs or dogs but I definitely did just at a later date. In my defense it was like one month into Covid so that also was a factor in my decision making!

Oh I forgot to mention the MAGA neighbor has been dropping off fresh baskets of produce for us as a neighborly gesture. Like overflowing cornucopias of greens and peppers and squash and shit. I guess we're friends now (?).

It's a lot better than constant tension sure but now I have to eat corn for dinner every night.

It's September and we went to a polling station at a school we've never been to and voted for the first time in this new town. There was only one contested election on our ballot today the primary between Joe Kennedy and Ed Markey and I filled in the little square next to the latter's name with a pen I was assured had been sanitized very vigorously and I went and slipped the ballot into the little machine they have while the old lady sitting there in the plastic face guard and cloth mask coughed a grim cough that didn't make me feel much like lingering. As we left one person was grazing by the table of donuts under the basketball hoop and when we got outside there was a playground and Michelle said that is such a sad-looking little playground but I thought it looked basically fine. Being a teacher she would know more about the playground standards of today than I would I suppose.

Another thing I did this week for the first time in over a decade was watch the movie *Jacob's Ladder* which I distinctly remember fucking me up as a kid and it occurred to me that a large chunk of all the films and books I read when I was young basically had the same lesson which was: Being in the Vietnam War Fucking Sucked Shit. And I believed them all. I believed it sucked a massive amount of shit and thankfully I never had to find out firsthand. I was just thinking about it and doing some math and I realized my father was probably just too young to have been made to go over there to kill and die and that seemed weird to me. It's a very basic fact of my life that I had never thought about that my father was too young to go die and kill in Vietnam. He got to die here in America instead so that's nice. My stepfather was old enough but I think he was playing football in college at the time and I'm sure he much preferred that to the alternative and I do not blame him.

There's a quote from *Jacob's Ladder* that has stuck with me for a long time and it's spoken by Danny Aiello's character with this smile that feels simultaneously comforting and menacing and you're not sure what his deal is like with everything else going on like whether he's a demon or what have you and it goes like this:

"If you're afraid of dying, and you're holding on, you'll see devils tearing your life away. But if you've made your peace, then the devils are really angels, freeing you from the world."

I am personally to be very clear here afraid of dying. If it happens any time soon I'm afraid it will be the devils for me.

The next day I met Michelle back in our old neighborhood and I thought I was going to feel something more than I did but it was just like we had left it minus you know . . . everything. We sat at a table outside on the sidewalk of our old pub and ordered the same things we used to order and talked about the new things we talk about now and I thought some of the servers or the guy at my old store I stopped in at after might ask us where we had been but they didn't seem to register that we weren't there because almost no one had been much of anywhere anymore except inside their homes. On the way out we drove by our old place you know how you do that and it's supposed to be this whole thing and all the lights were out and it didn't look like they had managed to rent it out to anyone yet it looked like everyone was gone.

I HAVE TO STOP

I have to stop this somewhere but every time I think I've said enough a year's worth of history happens the next day.

I know we've each said something like this about a hundred different things in the past couple of years but I don't think anything has made me feel like the bottom has fallen out more than the immediate lionization of Kyle Rittenhouse the vigilante boy who killed two people and injured a third in the streets of Kenosha, Wisconsin amidst the protests over the police shooting of Jacob Blake. Perhaps when I read that the police had handcuffed Blake to his hospital bed despite having paralyzed him by shooting him seven times in the back for nothing. That there was another particularly sickening and low moment for me and for all of us too. But this effort to turn Rittenhouse into a hero has been something to behold.

"How shocked are we that 17-year-olds with rifles decided they had to maintain order when no one else would?" Tucker Carlson said on his program the following night.

Numerous fundraisers popped up after the news broke last week including one on the "Christians for Christians" fundraising platform GiveSendGo which I just tried to log on to but it appears to be down perhaps because so many Christians are trying to send him cash.

"Kyle Rittenhouse just defended himself from a brutal attack by multiple members of the far-leftist group ANTIFA— the experience was undoubtedly a brutal one, as he was forced to take two lives to defend his own," they wrote. They had raised almost $200,000 for him last I saw. Hundred large a scalp.

A second fundraiser by a group called National Association for Gun Rights justified his shooting similarly.

"Kyle was doing his best to protect business owners from losing their entire livelihoods when criminal actors instigated violence against him," they said. "Unfortunately for them, Kyle was armed with an AR-15 and their rocks, skateboards, and handguns stood no chance against his well-placed shots."

Another effort was set up by the Arizona State University college Republicans group.

"Half of all funds collected this semester for Republicans United will be donated to 17-year-old Kyle Rittenhouse legal defense fund," they tweeted. "He does not deserve to have his entire life destroyed because of the actions of violent anarchists during a lawless riot."

All of which would be bad enough if it didn't inevitably coil its way through the sewers and up out through the plumbing into the brain of Donald Trump who not only refused to condemn the shooter when asked but in fact justified his actions.

"He was trying to get away from them I guess it looks like," he said. "And he fell. And then they very violently attacked him . . . I guess he was in very big trouble. He would have been, he probably would have been killed."

And to think all this time all of our other mass shooters could have just been doing shit like this and gotten a pass. They might have gone out and only killed two or three "Antifa thugs" at a go and they could have become right-wing celebrities overnight. Probably a bad precedent to set here! I wonder if any other potential vigilantes out there will consider the approval of Rittenhouse from the president and vast swaths of the right and think about trying something themselves?

One ridiculous idea I had earlier this summer and yes yes I know was that police might think to themselves they would go hm maybe we should stop brutalizing and killing people on camera if only just for a little while until everyone stops focusing on us. Even just as a cynical ploy to get people off their backs I thought but once again I was a complete dumb shit because that's a big part of the job for them after all being able to do the violence without consequences.

After the protests kicked off some of the cops white-knuckled it through murdering detox for like one half of a shift then said ah fuck it. They couldn't do it. They love this shit.

It's mid-August and there have only been twelve days this entire year where police did not kill someone. That's 751 people in a matter of 235 days.

At least help is on the way in the form of the Biden/ Harris ticket right? Toward the end of the month the duo was interviewed on ABC News.

"President Trump says that you want to defund the police. Do you?" Robin Roberts asked.

"No I don't," Biden said, laughing.

"I don't want to defund police departments. I think they need more help, they need more assistance, but that, look, there are unethical senators, there are unethical presidents, there are unethical doctors, unethical lawyers, unethical prosecutors, there are unethical cops. They should be rooted out," Biden later added.

"By the way, he proposes cutting a half a billion dollars of local police support," Biden added, seemingly referring to the Trump administration's proposed cuts to a federal program that helps hire more local law enforcement officers.

"We have to make it clear that this is about protecting neighborhoods, protecting people, everybody across the board," he said. "So the only guy that actually put in a bill to actually defund the police is Donald Trump."

It's September and Biden is trying to outflank Trump with his support from law enforcement and every TV lib is doing the "Who respects John McCain more" routine after it was reported the president called him and other dead military losers and my god I just don't think we are prepared for what is coming.

Nobody gives a shit about honor and decency or whatever how do they all not know this yet? Improve our fucking lives with money not the vapor of ideals. I'm not sure how many times we can say this but there is no moral line Trump can cross that will turn his base away from him. None. If he goes on TV and fucks the flag well then the flag was asking for it.

There is a very simple calculus at work among Trump supporters about the way he disrespects the troops: if you're a troop or cop who supports Trump then you're a real and authentic warrior priest demigod and if you don't you're a traitor. It's that simple. Their respect for these guys is contingent. Stop expecting consistency.

Meanwhile and elsewhere vast swaths of demoralized nonvoters know Trump sucks so so bad they just haven't heard enough from Biden about the ways he is going to help them survive.

I am not a politics genius or very smart in any other way but this seems like this most obvious thing to me and it's just dangling there: Improve people's lives. We've been saying it for years!

Oh well. Maybe next time. Time to clock in at the shit-eating factory (nonunion).

WHAT DO WE WANT

Say what you will about a devastating pandemic amidst a swelling civil rights movement but it's certainly made finding a parking spot in Boston's Back Bay a lot easier. It's September further into September than seems natural it could ever be in this never-ending March and the city feels something like alive. Not fully there mind you but like after you've been laid low and ill and someone comes in to check on you in bed and says oh it looks like you're getting some color back in your cheeks.

The sidewalks were relatively crowded and people were jogging and the skaters were falling and getting back up and falling again in the empty fountain and couples were lounging on the grass in front of Trinity Church in Copley Square and if it weren't for all the masks you might convince yourself it was any other beautiful late summer day in any other year.

There were to be clear decidedly fewer military vehicle convoys stationed along every block like the last time I was in this neighborhood earlier in the summer. Fewer bored troops dicking around on their phones protecting the silent empty streets and shuttered trendy shops from nothing.

- Over in the park a crowd of a couple hundred were gathered for a "Rally for Black Lives, Black Voices and Jacob Blake" and a young band were playing a joyous and funky rendition of "Come Together" at the foot of the church. I had forgotten how the sun reflected off the towering Hancock building like a mischievous child's magnifying glass and so I found shade on the grass and sat quietly and nodded as I caught strangers' eyes in the way we do now and I read the signs and the words printed on people's masks like "Good trouble" and "No tyrants" and "Pro-Black is not anti-white" and "Don't drink bleach" which seems like it was probably very funny at one point when that was a whole thing people were talking about. Around the perimeter of the park a protest group called Refuse Fascism a group that I had joined up with earlier in the summer were marching and chanting about the threat of Trump and I remembered something about those particular organizers' insistence on centering the president as the issue bothering me then and it bothered me again this time. Not that he's not making matters worse it just doesn't seem like taking down this one specific guy is going to fix all the problems at hand buddy.

It's a start I suppose.

As the music stopped a speaker took the microphone. "This pandemic has exposed the true reality of what living in America is like for Black and Brown people," Danny Rivera a young organizer with the group Civic Youth Summit said. In front of him artists were plastering dozens of posters on the ground of the most high-profile Black people killed by police this year.

There are four things right now affecting us as a nation and disproportionately affecting Black and Brown people

Rivera went on. COVID-19 and economic injustice and voter suppression and police brutality.

"This corrupt system wants to mess with our health, with our ability to produce wealth and provide for our families. They're kneeling on our necks and silencing our voices, and even making it difficult for us to vote. And they're killing us. We are in the middle of a genocide. They're killing us in the thousands. So many are dead as a result of the lack of leadership and accountability, and we don't even know all the names of those killed at the hands of police officers," he said and then all together we said out loud the names we did know.

"None of this stuff is new," he said. "Which is why we're here to say enough is enough."

A series of other speakers came up next and the music went on and after a while something dawned on me some lightness I was feeling and it was in part the infectious energy of the crowd but it was also this: For the first time I can remember at a protest or rally this summer or any other time for that matter there were no police anywhere in sight monitoring us or bothering anyone or beating anyone's heads in. It felt like at least for an hour or two a weight had been lifted. It felt like the type of world I'd like to live in.

LUKE O'NEIL has written for *Esquire, New York Magazine, The Guardian, The New York Times Magazine, The Washington Post, The Atlantic, Playboy, Slate, Vice,* and many other publications. He is the author of *Welcome to Hell World: Dispatches from the American Dystopia.*